FEBOLD FEBOLDSON

FEBOLD
FEBOLDSON

Tall Tales From
The Great Plains

Compiled By

PAUL R. BEATH

Illustrated By

LYNN TRANK

UNIVERSITY OF NEBRASKA PRESS • Lincoln

Library of Congress Catalog card number A62-8725

International Standard Book Number 0-8032-5012-6

First Bison Book printing, October, 1962

Most recent printing shown by first digit below:

       4   5   6   7   8   9   10

Manufactured in the United States of America

To

MOTHER AND DAD

FOREWORD

I first became aware of Febold Feboldson when stories about him were appearing regularly in the Gothenburg, Nebraska, *Times*. As I recall, this was in 1927 or 1928. About this time, or perhaps a little later, I myself began to contribute an occasional story to the *Times*. Mostly adaptations of what I had heard around town, these stories were always slanted to fit what I conceived to be Febold's character—an indomitable Swedish pioneer who could surmount any difficulty.

Don Holmes of the *Times*, who nursed Febold in his infancy and whose aid in collecting these stories I gratefully acknowledge, told me he had picked up the character from Wayne T. Carroll. A lumber dealer, Carroll wrote a weekly newspaper column under the name Watt Tell. Lumber magazines were the first to use Paul Bunyan; it seems obvious that Febold was patterned after the giant logger. The Swede, however, could never have become a lumber hero because there are so few trees on the

Great Plains. Instead, he wrestled with regional adversities which beset the early settlers—tornadoes, hostile Indians, drouths, extreme heat and cold, unsavory politicians and floods.

Because I have published Febold more widely than either of his other champions, Carroll and Holmes, I have been credited with creating him. I did not. Febold, the pioneer Swede, and all his nephews were in existence when I came upon the legend.

It seems that Febold, the fabulous uncle, had already gone to his reward by retiring to California, that Valhalla of all good middlewesterners. His exploits are recounted by someone who had known him "in the old days," usually by one of his nephews —Bergstrom Stromberg, Herebold Farvardson, Hjalmar Hjalmarson, Kjontvedt Peterson, and Eldad Johnson. For some reason, there was always a contemporary of Febold known only as Eldad Johnson's grandfather.

The only historical basis for any of these characters is that Olof Bergstrom is probably the prototype of Bergstrom Stromberg. Olof, a preacher in the old country, gave up the ministry to lead a band of Swedish immigrants to the new world. He is reputed to have founded Stromsburg and Gothenburg, both in the state of Nebraska. It is my opinion that Carroll had this man in mind, because tales of him were current when I was a boy.

The real Bergstrom had a most hectic career. He was a flashy dresser and a persuasive talker. On one of his periodic returns to the old country for a fresh band of immigrants, he married a Swedish singer of some talent. He worked for the Union Pacific selling railroad land to the incoming Swedes. He once killed a man, was tried for murder, and acquitted. Although he made a fortune, it is reported that he was penniless when he left Nebraska. He then made his home in Tennessee where he later died; I have been unable to learn the place of his burial.

About 1928, the stories of Febold Feboldson "caught on." Not only did Don Holmes write them, but contributions began coming in from *Times* readers, not only from Nebraska, but from other states as well. Year by year, more and more bits of narrative material fastened themselves to the Febold legend until today he seems securely established as an American legendary hero.

In selecting the stories printed in this book, I have chosen only those tales which are typical of the life lived on the Great Plains. A complete collection of all the available material would have been more honest and scientific perhaps; it would, no doubt, have also bored the reader and falsified the essential character of the hero.

This collection of tall tales, evolving around Febold, represents the lighter, even humorous, side of the pioneer plainsman's serious and often tragic struggle to wrest a living from a stubborn land.

In addition to Wayne Carroll, who first set Febold to paper, and Don Holmes, who has nurtured him these many years, I should like to acknowledge the aid and comfort of Miss Emily Schossberger, editor of the University of Nebraska Press, and Professors Louise Pound and L. C. Wimberly of the University faculty. Frederick L. Christensen has furnished a few stories which would otherwise have escaped my attention. And for the final revision of the manuscript I am indebted more than he knows to Gaylord Marr.

Washington, D. C., Christmas, 1947.   —P. R. B.

CONTENTS

FOREWORD   vii

OLOF BERGSTROM: SWEDISH PIONEER   1
     by Louise Pound

I   THE DISMAL RIVER   15

II   JUST WIND   30

III   REAL AMERICAN WEATHER   38

IV   GREAT GUNS AND LITTLE FISHHOOKS   44

V   DROUTH BUSTIN'   56

VI   THE DIRTYLEG INDIANS   66

VII   SNAKES ALIVE   75

VIII   THE COYOTE CURE   82

IX   THE MOST INVENTINGEST MAN   87

X   POST HOLES   99

XI   THE WINTER OF THE PURPLE SNOW   104

XII   ROCKS OF THE OX   110

XIII	PRAIRIE PESTS	113
XIV	CALIFORNIA — THIS WAY OUT	121
	NEBRASKA STRONG MEN *by Louise Pound*	137

Olof Bergstrom: Swedish Pioneer

by Louise Pound

Olof Bergstrom, an early settler in Dawson County, was a leader of Swedish immigrants in the Gothenburg region. It has often been remarked that his life and activities in the Nebraska of the later nineteenth and earlier twentieth centuries deserve at least partial chronicling.[1] Some day, if and when the history of the Scandinavian element in Nebraska is written, his will be a prominent place. Not only was he an influential colonizer; he was a colorful personality; and, before it is too late, some account of him should be made available. It is nearly too late now, for hardly anyone who knew him is yet alive. What information is to be had may well be brought together at the present time as a contribution to the history of Dawson County.

A German settlement preceded the Swedish in the Gothenburg locale. The Germans came mostly from the eastern states and they had in some degree resources to fall back on. They preempted the choicer locations for their homesteads. When the settlers from Sweden came, this in 1882, their alternatives were to homestead the less desirable land to the north and west of the present Gothenburg, or to buy land from the Union Pacific railroad, which had penetrated and crossed Nebraska by the late 1860's. The federal government gave the Union Pacific every

---

[1] For the suggestion that this article be written and for much or most of the information supplied I am indebted to P. R. Beath of Washington, D. C., and Don Holmes of the Gothenburg *Times*.

1

other section of land (the odd numbers) for ten miles on each side of the right of way. The railroad might then sell the surplus land to the settlers. Olof worked on the Union Pacific after coming to America in 1881 and he decided to homestead in the Gothenburg region, after a stay in the town of Stromsburg in Polk County of which his brother became a resident. He took his homestead in Dawson County in 1881. The original Bergstrom farmhouse was a dugout, the site a sheep pasture, and there was no house or building near. In the summer of 1882 a house of sun-dried brick was put up. The earlier farmhouse was used as a shelter for Swedish immigrants when they came until they were located on their own land.

Olof and the Plum Creek station agent, J. H. McColl, got the concession to sell land from the Union Pacific railroad. The railroad laid out eight blocks, now known as the Original Town, and built the first side track. The name Gothenburg given the site came from the Swedish city of Gothenburg (Göteborg) from which Olof had emigrated. In the spring of 1882 he went back to Sweden and induced a number of persons to come to Dawson County and to start the new town. He told them that they would soon be independent and he assured them that there was no need for them to learn English as this town would be made up of people from Sweden. When the Swedish settlers came in that same year, their alternatives, as already said, were to homestead the less desirable land north and west of the present Gothenburg or to buy land of the railroad at $6.00 an acre. More did the latter.

One of the Swedes coming in 1882 was Per Nelson, a preacher. He went again to Sweden and returned with another group of immigrants. He painted the Nebraska plains to them in glowing colors. Naturally those coming with him were disappointed when they found no town on arrival, but he told them to look forward to the future. Another of those coming from Sweden in 1882 was Dr. Vollrad Karlson. He worked in a Kearney drugstore, primarily as a pharmacist. The next spring he opened up his own drugstore in the second building to be built in Gothenburg, this in January, 1883. Dr. Karlson died while yet in his twenties; his was not a long life for one who played a large

2

part in the early days of Gothenburg. Two citizens of Gothenburg state that their impression is that Olof Bergstrom himself made several trips to Sweden, three perhaps, to bring more immigrants to Gothenburg and Dawson County.

The Gothenburg *Independent* of 1885 had an advertisement of Olof Bergstrom and Company.[2]

> The above firm is engaged in the real estate business, and is composed of O. Bergstrom, Dr. Vollrad Karlson and A. S. Booton. O. Bergstrom, then senior member of the firm, is a native of Sweden and came to America in 1881, making Nebraska his first permanent stopping place. He secured from the U. P. railroad six townships of land, the same including the present site of Gothenburg. He returned to Sweden sometime during the same year, but in 1882 he again set sail for America, bringing with him a party of about 370 of his countrymen. The major part of the company settled in Phelps County, but few caring to stake their fortunes in Gothenburg and vicinity—although a large number of them have since moved here. Mr. Bergstrom is the founder of Gothenburg and, having implicit faith in the future of the town, has labored zealously for its welfare.

His "implicit faith" was to be borne out, but probably, at the time he expressed it, it was more qualified than he represented to his followers. Elvina Karlson, daughter of Dr. Vollrad Karlson's brother Frederick, said in an interview in 1944, quoting her mother, that "knowing the hardships and slim pickings of the years ahead, Olof reasoned that only the Viking spirit of high courage and self reliance could hew a homestead out of this camping ground of Buffalo and Indians." In the same interview [3] Elvina Karlson told more that she had learned from the talk of her mother of Olof Bergstrom. Mrs. Frederick Karlson was his contemporary and knew him well.

In 1885 Mr. Bergstrom got up a petition for a Postoffice. The petition was accepted and Bergstrom was appointed Postmaster. Mail was brought to his house or homestead and anyone who wanted his mail called for it there. There was not

---

2 May 18, 1885.
3 Reported by P. R. Beath in 1944.

3

much mail, a sack coming in at a time. If no one was at the train to get the mail it was stuffed into a box used as a stepoff from the train. Sometimes the mail would remain there for days before some one from the Bergstrom's would walk down to get it. Bergstrom himself was seldom at home, newly arrived emigrants doing his work around the place. When the sack was brought back there was a general stampede for the key which hung on a nail, and the one getting the key was privileged to open the sack and dump it on the floor. The letters were then gathered and placed on a table. When people called for their mail they were invited to look through the mail on the table. In 1883 when Dr. Vollrad Karlson started his drugstore, the Post Office was moved there, on Front Street, and he served as mail clerk. Dr. Karlson conducted the Post Office in a more dignified manner. He went after the mail himself and tucked it away in a cigar box under the counter in the store. He sorted the letters and told the settlers if they had any mail.

Olof married a concert or opera singer as his second wife, and this seems to have had no little effect on his career. A soprano of considerable note, coming to this country from Sweden, she gave concerts in the East and had a wide repertory.

Inquiry sent to Mrs. J. A. Frawley, daughter of Lewis Headstrom, the founder of Stromsburg, brought the following information, in May, 1944. I am indebted for it to Chattie Westenius of Stromsburg, editor of the Stromsburg *Headlight*.

[As a child] I remember Olof Bergstrom's being spoken of as a revivalist type of Baptist preacher. . . . My parents attended some of these meetings, but he was never a guest at our house, either in Galva or Stromsburg. Then one day a letter came from him stating that he had just returned from Sweden and had attended a concert in Stockholm given by a beautiful and talented singer, and was told that she was very anxious to visit the U. S. A. and study for her career. So he conceived the idea that it might be a very profitable financial success if he could be her manager. He obtained an interview and arrangements were so made. He told her they would have to be married because in America it would not be proper for them to travel together except as man and wife. So they were married and lived at Gothenburg.

This is the account of her coming to America as told by Mrs. Bergstrom to Mrs. Frawley. The latter added that Bergstrom asked Mr. Headstrom to let his wife come to Stromsburg to give a concert, which she did, Mrs. Frawley playing her accompaniment. He had asked that the Headstroms sponsor her as their guest, and they did. This was about three years after Mrs. Frawley's marriage. Mrs. Frawley also remarked "Bergstrom's wife was a very pleasant and confiding guest but we never heard of either of them again."

The same issue of the Gothenburg *Independent* that printed the real estate advertisement of the Bergstrom-Karlson Company (May 16, 1895) contains, according to Don Holmes, "reports from Minneapolis papers about the Aklander-Bergstrom Concert Company of which Mrs. Bergstrom was the prima donna, with a soprano voice of remarkable strength, range and compass." Mrs. Frederick Karlson stated that "When they came back as bride and groom to Gothenburg, the Gothenburg band met the Bergstroms at the station, which was a platform merely with no building in sight as yet." Mrs. Bergstrom gave up concert singing. They lived in the home of sun-dried brick and entertained lavishly. In 1890 it became the scene of a killing.

Earlier Bergstrom had been deeply interested in temperance. According to Mrs. Karlson he even went to Sweden and organized there a Temperance Union called in Swedish *God Templar*. Finally, to continue Mrs. Karlson's testimony:

> Mrs. Bergstrom, forgetting her good training in Sweden and Olof Bergstrom falling a devotee of liquor, they carried on in their house extravagantly. A few of Mrs. Bergstrom's friends met there one evening. One of those present was a jolly sort of fellow, always teasing. He agitated Olof Bergstrom that night so that he picked up a revolver. There is no evidence to prove that he did shoot, or who did it, as all present were in the same state.

The last sentences refer to what was the most conspicuous event in Bergstrom's life in Dawson County, his trial for the murder of Ernest G. Edholm. Records concerning the case are on file in the office of the Clerk of the District Court in Lexington, Dawson County [4] and in the Appearance Docket. The killing took place March 14, 1890. The information against Bergstrom was filed March 15 by Edwin Edholm. The judge examined the following witnesses at the preliminary hearing: Dr. W. P. Smith, Annie Dell, Amanda Ingram for the complainant and Mrs. Sarah Johnson for the defendant. The defendant was represented by Hinman and Garret. The trial began June 9. The defendant with counsel appeared in court and pleaded not guilty. In the interval between July 9 and July 14, the jury was decided on. The papers in the case that are existent tell of formal motions made by the parties concerned and preserve three sketches of the scene of the crime and a few subpoenas. There is no verbatim testimony and the motive of the crime is nowhere mentioned.

For a transcription of the charge (The State of Nebraska, Dawson County, in the District Court of the Tenth Judicial District vs. Olaf Bergstrom), I am indebted to Mr. and Mrs. Frank Johnson of Lexington. I hope I may be pardoned for printing a section of the document. It is more interesting, perhaps, as a sample of the legal language of the time (legal language is said to be much simplified today) than as throwing light on the Bergstrom case. The italics, punctuation and spellings of the original have been retained.

Be it remembered that T. L. Warrington, County Attorney in and for Dawson County, and in the Tenth Judicial District of the State of Nebraska, who prosecutes in the name and by the Authority of the State of Nebraska, comes here in person into the Court at this June term, A. D. 1890 thereof and for the State of Nebraska gives the Court to *understood* and be informed that Olaf Bergstrom late of the County of Dawson, on the *Fourteenth* day of March, A. D. 1890 in the County of Dawson aforesaid in and upon one Ernest G. Edholm, then and there being unlawfully, purposely and feloniously and of deliberate and premeditated malice, did make an assault with the intent him the said Ernest G. Edholm unlawfully, purposely and of deliberate and premeditated malice to kill and

---

[4] District Court Journal, 3, pp. 100, 123, 140, 141; Appearance Docket, 2, p. 237.

murder, that the said Olaf Bergstrom, a certain rifle then and there charged with gun powder, and one leaden bullet, which the said rifle, he the said Olaf Bergstrom, in both of his hands, then and there had and held, then and there unlawfully, feloniously, purposely and of deliberate and premeditated malice, did discharge and shoot off, to, at, against and upon the left breast of the body of the said Ernest G. Edholm, and that the said Olaf Bergstrom with the leaden bullet aforesaid, out of the rifle aforesaid, then and there by the force of the gun powder, by the said Olaf Bergstrom, discharged and *shott* off as aforesaid, then and there, unlawfully, feloniously, purposely and of his deliberate and premeditated malice did strike, penetrate and wound, with the intent aforesaid thereby then and there, giving to the said Ernest G. Edholm, in and upon the left breast of the body of him, the said Ernest G. Edholm, then and there with the bullet aforesaid, so as aforesaid discharged and shot out of the rifle aforesaid by force of the gunpowder aforesaid by the said Olaf Bergstrom, in and upon the left breast of the body of him, the said Ernest G. Edholm, one mortal wound of the depth of four inches and the width of which said mortal wound, he the said Ernest G. Edholm instantly died, and the said T. L. Warrington, County Attorney, as aforesaid upon the authority aforesaid does say that the said Olaf Bergstrom, him, the said Ernest G. Edholm, unlawfully, feloniously, purposely and of his deliberate and premeditated malice did kill and murder contrary to the form of the Statute in such case made and provided and against the peace and dignity of the State of Nebraska.

T. L. Warrington, County Attorney

The following persons were named as jurors: Charles Cook, Thomas Patton, J. P. Cahow, J. B. Donaldson, Howard Koch, John Lee, Ed Thomlinson, William Reed, George Bogett, Con Hammond, William Tallowell, Jer Kearns, who were duly impaneled and sworn according to law. They returned their verdict in writing as follows:

We, the jury in this case, being duly impaneled and sworn in the above entitled case do find and say that we find the defendant not guilty,

J. P. Cahow, Foreman

7

And therefore it is ordered and adjudged that said defendant Olaf Bergstrom be discharged.

A statement made by Howard Koch, one of the last jurors to survive, concerning the trial of Olof Bergstrom is of interest.[5] Koch was born in Philadelphia, he states, in 1865. His father homesteaded north of Lexington and Howard came from Philadelphia to join him in 1877. Koch said:

> One day in the spring of 1880 I came to town to get some repairs for my binder. The sheriff met me on the street. He said to me:
>
> "Hello, Howard. The judge wants to see you."
>
> "Not me," I said. "I ain't got no time to serve on any jury. My binder is one of the best in the country and I've got to get it fixed."
>
> "Well, come on in anyway," said the sheriff.
>
> So I went in the court house and there they were preparing for the trial of Olaf Bergstrom for shooting that fellow up in Gothenburg. Well, the judge picked me for one of the jury, and I guess I'm the only one of them left.
>
> Well, I had heard of Bergstrom before the trial, but I had never seen him till that day. He was a partner of Jack McColl. I bought my farm from McColl.
>
> As for the trial itself, as best I can remember, the testimony was that Bergstrom and this fellow Edholm were sitting there on the settee in Bergstrom's house examining Bergstrom's goose-gun. We called shotguns "goose-guns" in those days; the country was full of geese. Well, they got to quarreling about the gun and finally to wrestling and it went off and shot Edholm and killed him. Bergstrom said Edholm was one of his best friends. I remember one of the lawyers tried to bring in about this fellow fooling around Bergstrom's wife, but he didn't get anywhere with that line. His wife was at the trial and seems to me she testified the same as her husband did. I remember too, about a Swedish maid the Bergstroms had, but she wasn't at the trial. Right away after the killing, I believe, she went back to Sweden.
>
> Well, there was only one thing to do, so we set him free. He was a big man, fine looking and wore a moustache. We all wore moustaches in those days.

5 Reported by P. R. Beath, 1944.

And after the trial, you know what? Bergstrom was so happy he took us into the back room and opened a little black bag he had and gave us each a $20 bill. Well, the trial was over, you understand, and he was happy to get free and wanted to do something for us.

According to Don Holmes, when the verdict came Olof Bergstrom was met at the train by the Gothenburg Silver Cornet Band and escorted to his home.

The best account of Bergstrom was obtained by P. R. Beath from Mrs. Frederick Karlson, Sr. It should be printed in full. It was written down in 1944 by Miss Elvina Karlson of Gothenburg from the conversation of her mother, Mrs. Frederick Karlson, Sr. A few sentences from it have been quoted in preceding pages.

I arrived in Gothenburg, Nebraska, the morning of June 18, 1885. In the afternoon I went to my brother's drugstore. Outside was Olof Bergstrom standing by his team of horses and buggy. He was all dressed up for the occasion to meet Dr. Vollrad's sister who had just arrived from Sweden. Dr. Vollrad Karlson was secretary to Olof Bergstrom and Company. Olof Bergstrom was a very handsome gentleman, fine physique, six feet tall, brown curly hair. He was dressed in a dark suit, white shirt, white vest. He was outstanding in his mannerisms. One characteristic was he always held his head on one side and had a pleasant smile. He possessed a fine personality. He spoke excellent Swedish; he was a Swedish minister from Göteborg, Sweden. He did not use much English because he contacted mostly Swedish people. His parents were very fine folks in Sundsvall, Sweden.

He lived in Göteborg, Sweden, before he came to America in 1880. He first went to Stromsburg, then to Gothenburg in 1881. He was a Real Estate agent for the Union Pacific railroad; he sold railroad land cheap. He was in the real estate business, sold railroad land and was agent for the homestead land. He was no relation to McColl. Mr. McColl, an attorney, was real Estate Agent at Plum Creek, Lexington, Nebraska, for the Union Pacific Railroad Company. Mr. Bergstrom would consult Mr. McColl on the many land deals. Bergstrom was no relation to E. G. West. They were business partners. Mr. West came with Mr. Bergstrom from Chicago.

9

He told them [his recruits in Sweden] that land was so cheap that they would soon be very independent. They would not have to learn to speak the English language because there would be just Swedes from Sweden. They could possess their own beautiful valley, he said, "the wonderful Platte Valley, the greatest agricultural valley in the world excepting the Nile in Egypt." To homeseekers he made the statement "The Early Bird Catches the Worm."

He was married twice, would have been married the third time but he left the bride "waiting at the church." His first wife was a very cultured woman. He had a beautiful daughter by this marriage. The daughter had a winning personality like her father. She studied music in Boston and Chicago. Mr. Bergstrom played the violin very well. The daughter died at the young age of twenty-five years; she grieved so much over the loss of her father's speculations in Chicago. His second wife was very homely but a fine dresser. She was an opera singer from Stockholm, Sweden. She sang in grand opera there. She received her education there. She gave concerts at the cities and towns in America. A pianist from Boston was her accompanist. Mr. Bergstrom's plans were that she would make a great deal of money with her mezzo soprano voice. I'm sorry to say Mrs. Bergstrom did not use her career to a good end. She died in the County Hospital at Omaha and sold her body for medical purposes.

Olaf Bergstrom was tried for murder but acquitted. The jury decided that under the circumstances Bergstrom could not be accused alone, because the other men in the party were drunk as well as Bergstrom. A minister from the East pleaded this case to this ending.

In later life Bergstrom lost all his wealth, probably through speculations in Chicago, and went to Tennessee. The late Ernest Calling who came to Gothenburg in 1889 and was at one time a partner of Bergstrom told P. R. Beath, July, 1944, that he bought the farm immediately north of Lake Gothenburg from Olof Bergstrom in 1906. This farm was the scene of the killing for which Bergstrom was tried and acquitted. Later Bergstrom returned from Tennessee and wanted Calling to trade for some Tennessee land the farm where he intended to spend his last days. Calling refused and Bergstrom returned to Tennessee. It was probably of the same occasion that Mrs. Karlson said, according to the account of her daughter in 1944, "Mr. Bergstrom lost all his wealth and returned the last time plain 'broke.' He went to Mr. Karlson's market and wanted to pawn his watch and chain, but Mr. Karlson said 'No.' He fixed up a nice lunch of meat, crackers and cheese etc. for Bergstrom. Olof's many friends helped him. He left for Tennessee and died there."

An article on Bergstrom is said to have appeared in the Chicago newspaper *Svenska Amerikanaren Tribunen.* Whether this was before or after his death I do not know. Elvina Karlson was unable to obtain from the newspaper the date of the issue in which it is supposed to have been printed.

In a few respects tales and anecdotes of Olof Bergstrom have affiliations with Nebraska folklore. When I first looked into his history I thought there must be something of legend associated with his attitude toward strong drink. Various sources of information mentioned him as almost a fanatic crusader for Temperance. Other sources mentioned his unique prowess as a drinker. My brother Roscoe, for instance, whose remarkable memory is well known, recalls stories of Olof's prodigious capacity as regards alcoholic potations. But in due time I realized that folklore was not involved in these contradictory reports. Both accounts of his attitude seem to have been true. A preacher, he started life in the United States as a strong advocate of temperance. Perhaps it was after his marriage to the opera singer that he surrendered to the attraction of alcoholic beverages, serving them liberally in his home and drinking with others as the custom was. The representations of Mrs. Karlson are relevant here and no doubt should be accepted. His change of attitude was fact; no lore entered into it. Beyond question, however, is Olof's relation to the folk stories of Febold, the Nebraska strong man. Paul R. Beath, editor of *Febold Feboldson: Tall Tales of the Great Plains* (1948), states that Febold was a reconstruction of Olof Bergstrom, though the name got itself applied to or mixed up with Bergstrom Stromsberg, the reputed grandnephew of Febold and the narrator of tall tales concerning him. The same testimony is given by Don Holmes of the Gothenburg newspaper in which many of these tales were originally printed

11

and are still being printed. Olof played, then, a leading part in the genesis of the Nebraska Febold tales. A third bit of lore that has a degree of circulation by chroniclers of Febold is that, by transposition of syllables, the town of Stromsburg was named from Bergstrom. Olof's brother Andrew became a resident of Stromsburg, as mentioned already, but the town was founded by Lewis Headstrom in 1872, nearly a decade before Olof came to the United States. According to the historian of the place,[6] it took its name not from Olof Bergstrom but from its earliest inhabitant, Headstrom, *-burg* being added to the second syllable of his name (*Strom's burg*). The same explanation is given in *Nebraska Place-Names*.[7] Unmistakably the association of Olof Bergstrom with the naming of Stromsburg is folklore.

Reprinted from *Nebraska History*, XXXI (March, 1950), 64-74.

---

[6] Chattie Westenius, *History of Stromsburg* (Stromsburg, 1931), p. 2.

[7] Lilian Fitzpatrick, *Nebraska Place-Names,* (University of Nebraska, 1925), p. 117.

FEBOLD FEBOLDSON

CHAPTER ONE

THE DISMAL RIVER

When and how Febold Feboldson came to the Great Plains, and particularly to Nebraska, is one of the most controversial issues about the mighty Swede.

Febold—if one can believe the tales by Bergstrom Stromberg, a grand-nephew of the fabulous plainsman—was born in the south of Sweden many years ago. He came to America with a bag of meager belongings under his right arm; under his left arm was Eldad Johnson's grandfather—asleep as usual.

According to Bergstrom's calculations, the day Febold hit Nebraska must have been one of the hottest in the history of the state. Nebraska, in those days, was bounded on the north and south by a continuance of the Rocky Mountains. That summer, because of the intense heat, the jagged peaks melted and ran. A sudden hailstorm chilled them so that they remained with rounded tops and later topographers considered them foothills. Farther north, the sudden chilling crumbled the rocks and the huge blisters which bubbled up under the great heat burst and pitted the land with sand pockets and blowouts.

Febold, who had the stamina of a twenty-mule team in an alkali desert, pressed on with boundless enthusiasm, anxious to get to the Rocky Mountains and eventually to California. Eldad, however, could not take it. The heat, the glaring sky, and the monotonous stretches of grass unsettled his mind. When thin smoke crinkled skyward from their banked campfire at night, he dreamed of Sweden—the cool lakes, the mist-green pines that covered the hills, the sheltered and unworried happiness he had known there. During the day, he continually saw mirages of shimmering water which receded as he advanced toward them.

On one particularly hot afternoon, he shouted and pointed: "Look, look—water!"

Febold followed his finger. Sure enough, a wide ribbon of tawny water gleamed just ahead.

"What a dismal river," Febold remarked disdainfully, and prepared to move on.

"I don't care if it *is* dismal," shouted Eldad desperately. "Let's stay here—until winter anyway. Please, Febold! Go ahead—call it the dismal river, better dismal than none at all."

With a wild cry, Eldad ran like a maniac, shedding his clothes. He held his nose and dived headfirst into the deceptively shallow water. His head and shoulders stuck in the silt of the river bed. Febold grabbed his feet and pulled him from the soft mud.

Poor Eldad's neck was broken—but not beyond repair. That settled it. They would have to stay on the Dismal River until Eldad's neck mended.

To speed the recovery of his friend, Febold snared wild fowl to make invigorating broth and tasty morsels from the birds roasted on a spit over their campfire.

A real delicacy was the so-called "Mugwump" bird, an aviarian oddity so physically constructed that one could not differentiate between the head and the tail—they looked the same. The name was derived from the bird's habit of sitting on fences with his mug on one side and his wump on the other. The birds, a recent scientific study indicates, were often undecided themselves which end was which, and sometimes started to fly away in opposite directions. The resultant worry and strain is thought to have led to their disappearance.

Mosquitoes, in those days, attained gargantuan proportions. Febold made this discovery the first night he camped near the Dismal River. Awakened by what he believed was the sound of riveters, the Swede investigated and found it was merely the good old prairie mosquito at work.

Warned by an ominous droning, Febold glanced skyward and was startled to see a fleet of mosquitoes bearing down on him. The Swede armed himself with a small but heavy hammer and took cover inside an iron boiler lashed to his covered wagon. After reconnoitering for several minutes, the mosquitoes decided that the only way to get at him was to go in after him. Droning noisily, the insects attacked the boiler. As fast as they stuck their stingers through its iron sides, Febold clinched their stingers

17

with his hammer. Soon the entire fleet was helpless, unable to pull their stingers from the boiler. Febold climbed outside and finished them off with a blast from his muzzle-loading shotgun; he had brought the weapon along as a protection against bears.

This experience led to Febold's invention of mosquito netting. The netting he invented, however, was made of steel wire and was the forerunner of the hail screen used nowadays. Modern mosquito netting was not adopted until years after the country had become better civilized.

Febold's decision to make his home near the Dismal River was complicated by the fact that in those days there were no surveyors to plat the land one wished to homestead.

Because Eldad Johnson's grandfather was still recuperating from his broken neck, Febold decided to settle near the scene of his friend's unfortunate accident. Typical of Febold's ingenuity was the unique method he devised for staking out his claim:

He breathed deeply and ran as far as he could without taking another breath. There he drove a stake. Then starting at right angles to the imaginary line he had just staked, he repeated the procedure until he had his four sides staked out.

There was one difficulty with this idea, however. Febold ran uphill on the south line. That line, when measured later, was eighteen miles long; the other lines were only a few hundred yards above ten miles. The giant plainsman quickly rectified his error. He plowed a furrow along each side of his boundary line and, finding that they did not meet, he just took a good hold of one furrow and pulled it out straight to meet the others as he had intended.

The Swede's attempt to use a similar plan years later when he was helping with the laying of the Union Pacific resulted in the first railroad wreck on the new line.

Because Nebraska, in those days, was a treeless expanse or prairie, Febold realized that he would have to find trees in another locale if he were to build the log cabin he contemplated. The hardy pioneer started west and walked to the Redwood Forest in California before he found trees which he considered suitable. Febold picked a dozen choice trees, pulled them up by their roots, tied them securely with a huge log chain, and started back to Nebraska. When he got home, he was astounded to discover that the treetops had worn themselves out from being dragged halfway across the continent. Even to this day, one can still see stretches of red soil and sand between California and Nebraska. Those Redwood trees were ground to powder as Febold dragged them along.

He simply shrugged and said, "Oh, well, live and learn." However, he did regret that he had wasted three days walking to and from California for nothing but a dozen tree stumps.

Febold lost almost a day on his trip to California because he went miles out of his way to the south to escape the deep snow and bitter cold of the Rocky Mountains. While passing through what is now Arizona, the Swede stopped in a great forest to examine the lumber, hoping that it might prove suitable for the cabin he was about to build. Febold, as finicky as a kitten in a catnip patch, found the trees unsatisfactory. After deciding to leave the forest, he discovered that he had lost his sense of direction.

The thought that he, Febold Feboldson, greatest of all woodsmen and plainsmen, was lost as though he were an ordinary tenderfoot, was more than his pride could bear. Beserk with rage, the angry Swede tore up tree after tree by its roots. After he had cleared a pathway and discovered his directions, Febold looked back at the once-beautiful forest. It was now a tangle of shattered stumps and twisted foliage. Febold surveyed his destruction with sickening heart, his tantrum leaving him as fast as it had begun. He slunk away, ashamed of his childishness.

Natives of the country called it "The Pulverized Forest of Febold," but the name was gradually corrupted until it became simply "The Petrified Forest."

When Febold first came to Nebraska, it was a part of the region known as "The Great American Desert" or "The Treeless Prairie." Convinced that both names were derogatory and insulting, Febold instituted a practice for which a latter day Nebraskan became famous—tree planting.

The Swede started out with cottonwood seeds. He dug holes and planted them carefully—at first; but he had a lot of seeds and a lot of places in which to plant them. Soon he became very tired of his task and, instead of planting the seeds, he simply tossed them by handfuls down prairie dog holes. This accounts for the many cottonwood groves scattered across the state.

The first spring Febold spent in the state was inordinately dry and the Swede, for a while, carried water to his trees. Then he, like most midwesterners, succumbed to spring fever. He let the cottonwoods go and planted willows, instead, along the Dismal River so he would not have to carry water during the dry summer that was sure to follow.

The large number of willows bordering the river and creeks in Nebraska where there is plenty of water are ample evidence of Febold's early interest in planting trees. However, the creeks and streams dry up every summer.

Like most of the early settlers who pioneered Nebraska, Febold lived in a "soddie" the first year he homesteaded. Wishing a more substantial dwelling, the Swede cut timber from the trees he had planted and built the first structure with a basement in architectural history. This remarkable feat was one of those amazing accidents which, like so many others, later proved a boon to mankind.

Febold built a log shanty. One night a strong wind came up and blew the sand out from under it; the next morning the top of the shanty was level with the ground. Undaunted, Febold built another cabin on top of the buried one, using its roof for

21

the floor of his second house. A Hercules at housebuilding, Febold finished his second cabin in one day. The next morning when he awoke, he was astounded to see that the wind had again blown the sand from under the foundation of his house. When he built his third cabin on top, he found that the other two cabins underneath had settled so far that he had running water in the bottom one. Febold finally built a wind break, but the sand blew out from under it, and the next day he had to rebuild it. At last he discovered a way to anchor his windbreak, and took out patents on the first sky-hook arrangement. The hooks held the wind in place and stopped the undermining of his cabins.

It was thus that the basement and more-than-one-story house evolved from Febold's tenacity to beat a wind that misbehaved.

One of the most spectacular furnishings in Febold's new house was a clock with a great, swinging pendulum enclosed in a polished wooden cabinet. Brought west over the Allegheny mountains, the timepiece had belonged to his grandfather in Sweden; Febold's frequent references to it as "grandfather's clock" led to all timepieces of that variety being known by that name.

But anyway, the clock was a huge affair and it was given the place of honor in the corner by the fireplace. Febold was a stickler for order. He believed that there was a place for everything, and everything should be in its place. Once he arranged the furniture in his house, there it stayed.

The grandfather's clock remained in the corner for a number of years, never missing a tick, the heavy pendulum swinging back and forth with metronomic regularity. The pendulum—that's where the trouble came in—was really a heavy thing. It cast a shadow which gradually wore into the wall of the room until it actually weakened the structure of the building. This corner of the house projected out over a hillside; one day it collapsed and carried the whole building crashing to the bottom of a canyon.

Febold was chagrined, to say the least. Delving into his junk box, he constructed a watch so tiny that it was too small to carry in his pocket. Because he kept misplacing it, he got a piece of cord and tied it onto his wrist. Thus Febold invented the first wrist watch and became the godfather of the jewelry business.

While Febold was establishing his ranch on the Dismal River, he was cut off from mankind for months at a time. On those rare occasions when he left his homestead and went into the little trading post on Plum Creek for supplies, the Swede was prone to "put on a party."

The first place he headed for, after out-spanning his forty-ox team and turning them out to graze, was a saloon where he whet his appetite with a half-gallon of good red likker. After this apertif, Febold lumbered across the street to The Eggy Fork restaurant. With a huge platter of wild turkey eggs in front of him—flanked by a whole ham, a peck of roasted potatoes, a size-able roast of buffalo or b'ar's meat, a few loaves of cracklin' bread, and enough strong coffee to wash it all down—Febold embarked on his spree.

The result of one of his orgies was that the local inhabitants were forced to go on short rations until the arrival of the next freight outfit from St. Joe.

The first winter Febold spent in the state was a rigorous one. Snow fell to the depth of ten feet and completely covered the entire Louisiana Purchase. The Swede invented a snow-plow to open the trails and relieve the suffering of the Indians. The plow was a giant wedge designed to toss the snow up on either side; a high seat for Febold enabled him to oversee the workings of his invention. He made a huge harness and had all of the neighboring Indians hooked up and ready to go. When the Indians saw that Febold was going to sit on the seat and not push, they refused to cooperate. Instead, they sat stubbornly in the snow; this was the first incident of frozen assets and the first sit-down strike in history.

Undaunted, Febold put on his snowshoes, got his lariat, and took a walk over the frozen drifts. Discovering a herd of buffalo trapped in the snow where they had broken through the crusty surface, the Swedish pioneer lassooed the beasts, pulled them from the drifts in which they were floundering, and harnessed them to his snow plow. Tense with the excitement of the moment, the entire tribe of Indians whooped suddenly. Startled by the Indian cries and thinking they were about to be slaughtered, the buffaloes stampeded. Away they went, plunging and leaping madly through the drifts. It was all Febold could do to hang onto the leather lines and keep his seat.

When the buffaloes finally dropped from exhaustion near the Missouri River, Febold thanked his lucky stars that he had been fortunate enough to escape with his life. On the way back to his cabin, he discovered that he had set his plow a little too deep.

With the spring thaw, the melted snows filled the path of the snowplow, widening as the amount of water increased. A perpetual reminder of Febold's ill-fated escapade, the remaining river was called the Platte, which means, in Indian dialect, "the wagon-that-digs-a-ditch-in-the-ground."

In the meantime, gold had been discovered in California, and many wagon trains headed west were caught in the deep snows that covered Nebraska. Instead of thawing with the coming of spring, the snows remained throughout the summer until the next winter when more snow fell; the phenomenon was called the Year of the Petrified Snow. As a result of Nebraska's inhospitable weather, the '48ers were held up in their gold rush and became '49ers.

At that time Febold was operating an ox train between San Francisco and Kansas City because the snow prevented him from doing anything else. Since he was the only plainsman able to withstand the winter weather that year, the '48ers appealed to him for help. His secret was to load his wagon with sand from Death Valley, California; neither he nor his oxen grew cold because the sands of the desert never lost their heat. He sold this sand to the gold rushers at fifty dollars a bushel. It was really a preposterous price but the frozen prospectors were glad to pay it.

In January, 1849, the prospectors began their westward trek over the snow-covered plains in their prairie schooners. Before they reached the Rockies, however, the jolting of the wagons had scattered the sand and covered every bit of the Petrified Snow. That's the reason, according to Bergstrom Stromberg who handed down this tale of the fabulous Febold, that the prairies are so all-fired hot in the summertime.

Febold cursed himself twenty times a day for the next twenty years for selling the '48ers that torrid sand. He spent the next twenty years attempting various schemes to moderate the climate. Deciding nothing could be done about Nebraska weather, the Swede went to California. But that's another story.

Few people realize, Bergstrom Stromberg declares, that his great-uncle Febold was one of the first people to perceive the need for settling the state. The Swede's expert knowledge of fishing came in handy in his great fight against the pernicious influence of the gold hunger in California.

The mischievous malady threatened to depopulate the nation. Febold was peeved to see California draining the people and money from the rest of the country.

Since the prospectors were seeking gold, Febold had a scheme for the discovery of the precious metal in the rivers of the Great Plains. He stocked the streams with Peruvian moulting goldfish. This species, now extinct, deceived the Spanish conquistadors during their conquest of the Inca empire in Peru; the fish shed their golden scales every Wednesday of every week except during leap year. Every fourth year the fish moult every other week—a phenomenon which science has yet failed to explain.

Febold's plan worked better than he had anticipated. Soon the river beds of the Platte, Republican and other Nebraska streams were as brilliant as a Californian's account of his adopted state. The minute a '49er saw this golden glitter he would unsling his dishpan and go to work.

Febold finally decided it was no use trying to hold them. The prospectors, worn out with work and disillusioned, departed for California anyway—after 40 or 50 years.

It was the year that the United States government consulted Febold about establishing a Nebraska-Kansas boundary line that Febold first met Paul Bunyan. The two had been asked by the Federal authorities to re-establish the state line. That was right after Paul had leveled Kansas; before that, the state had been the most mountainous in the country. Paul, with the aid of Babe, the Blue Ox, turned the peaks over and, just as he expected, found them flat on the bottom. But in leveling the state, he accidently erased the northern boundary line between the two states; no one could tell where Kansas ended and Nebraska began.

Since neither Paul nor Febold could read or operate surveying instruments, they were forced to rely on their wits. The giant logger admitted that he made a mess of the job by trying to plow a furrow from Colorado to Missouri. The resultant channel, filled with spring thaws and rainwater, became what is now known as the Republican river. Although the river is nearly parallel with the state line, it is, of course, very crooked in some places and too far north.

Then, too, the government did not wish to use the Republican River as a boundary—that would be unfair to the Democrats. Febold accused Paul of being drunk, but after it was explained that Kansas was a dry state, the big Swede admitted that it is almost impossible to make a straight line without the use of mechanical aid. Almost, but not quite. Febold would never admit anything was impossible.

He began to experiment with eagles and bumble bees. After fifteen years, he finally succeeded in breeding bees as large as eagles. He hitched one of his huskiest specimens to a plow and plowed a bee-line for a boundary. The state line was re-established and Febold again proved that nothing is impossible.

CHAPTER TWO

JUST WIND

The first question a stranger asks when he visits the Great Plains is "Does the wind blow this way all the time?" The native always answers "No, sometimes it blows harder." That is, the average native makes this reply; Bergstrom Stromberg would undoubtedly tell the stranger the story of the musical wind.

At a rally of old-timers up his way, Bergstrom was asked which he considered the worst for the country: grasshoppers, drouths, floods, tornadoes, Congress or Wall Street. As everyone expected him to name one of the last two, it was quite a surprise when Stromberg unhesitatingly declared that the musical wind was the most demoralizing thing which ever hit the Great Plains.

It came during one of the presidential years. Bergstrom is not sure which one because his great-uncle Febold neglected to tell him when he related the story. Anyway, about the first of August, just when the farmers were beginning to harvest the biggest bumper crop in years, a cool breeze suddenly sprang up from the East. The men harvesting were glad to cool off. As soon as they relaxed, they began to hear music everywhere—old-time circle two-steps, hoe-downs and square dances.

Harvesting was over then and there. Everyone began dancing and singing to the musical wind. It lasted until the second Wednesday in November and then stopped as suddenly as it had begun. Word came from the East that Wall Street had again gained control of the country.

Febold always had a sneaking suspicion that the politicians had started the musical wind to keep the farmers' minds off the election.

Mention of the prairie's unpredictable wind always reminds Herebold Farvardson, another of Febold's nephews, of the time Eldad Johnson's grandfather was blown off his windmill. He lit on his stomach, the wind knocked clean out of him, Herebold recollects. Efforts to revive the old man proved useless and his neighbors, naturally, thought him dead.

Sorry beyond words at his companion's apparent departure from this vale of tears, Febold built a coffin and notified the relatives that the funeral would be held the next day.

The funeral procession had gotten only halfway to the grave-yard when a forty-mile wind hit the crowd and blew everybody back to the old home place. When Febold started to look for the remains of his friend, he was astounded to see Eldad Johnson's grandfather climb down off the windmill. The wind had blown life back into him as well as blowing him back on the mill.

The only thing the old man said to Febold when he reached the ground was: "That consarned wind sure is fierce today, ain't it?"

Kite flying during the March winds has always been a favorite Great Plains pastime. Febold Feboldson was one of the first plainsmen to indulge in this sport.

Once the Swede built a huge kite, so large that it needed rope instead of string. He tied one end to a tree and was watching his kite climb into the air when the knot began to pull loose. Febold grabbed the end of the rope just as it became untied, and the next thing he knew a strong wind had seized the kite and pulled him with it into the air.

His weight proved the perfect balance for the kite. It rose to a great height where the wind was chill and very strong. Dismayed, and more frightened than he would admit, Febold began to wonder when, if ever, he would get back to earth. Then he had a bright idea! He took a slingshot from his pocket and began to put pebbles through the kite. After he had shot the same number of holes through each side—to keep the kite on an even keel—it began to lose altitude; when it got lower where the wind was weaker, the kite plummeted downward at an alarming rate of speed.

Febold's quick thinking again came to his assistance. He removed his shirt and the wind carried it up against the kite; the kite, however, was so large it took all the clothing Febold had on to keep it afloat. When it got low enough, the Swede dropped

32

uninjured into the upper branches of a huge tree. Unable to locate the kite or his clothes (he learned later that the kite finally came down in what is now North Dakota), Febold had a long tramp back and a number of tough explanations to make to the Indians whom he encountered on his way home.

Love, or sentimentality of any sort, was about the last thing in the world one would associate with Febold. Surely, though, the old codger must have had his moments; or perhaps Bergstrom Stromberg colored with sentiment a story which his great-uncle used to tell each spring when the first warm winds from the south began to give everyone spring fever.

It seems that one day in early spring Febold was walking in his pasture on the Dismal River. The Swede, dressed for the beguiling warmth that tanged the air, suddenly felt a cold wind on the back of his neck. He turned and, sure enough, a Canadian blizzard was howling toward him from the northwest hills. Febold ducked into a sandhill blowout, expecting the storm to pass as quickly as it had come.

Instead of going about its business, the blizzard lingered in the vicinity. Febold thought this most unusual; then he noticed a spring breeze skipping over the hills from the south. Watching with interest, he wondered whether he was about to witness a rendezvous or an ambush.

When she saw the Canadian blizzard, the spring breeze stopped, undecided whether to advance or to retreat. The blizzard ruffled his frosty hair, thumped his chest in a gesture of defiance, and began to show off. After whirling a skift of snow across the hills, he whipped the white into fantastic drifts. This was followed by a rattle of hail and another flurry of flakes. Febold, in the meantime, was nearly buried in snow.

The poor little spring breeze blushed with becoming femininity at this display of masculine vigor. As the blizzad came closer, she fluttered her zephyrs and swooned in his arms. The north wind placed his frosty fingers on her brow and the spring breeze revived. The Canadian blizzard proposed marriage and the spring breeze accepted. They whirled off together, with their arms about one another.

Febold heard afterward that they had gone off to Kansas to start a small tornado business.

According to Bergstrom Stromberg and other old-timers, the Louisiana Purchase used to be the breeding place for tornadoes. Several times daily twisters ripped and tore up and down the country until both settlers and the native Indians feared for their lives.

Febold took it upon himself to rid the region of these storms. Each time he saw unruly clouds form the funnel shape that characterized tornadoes, he dashed out with his trusty lariat, captured the clouds, and tied them up until their force was spent. As the cyclonic winds got wise to Febold, they attempted to outrun or circle around him. The huge plainsman, however, chased them away, frequently driving them over the Mexican border. Before long the storms were afraid to cross the line.

Learning that Febold is now in California, the tornadoes have sneaked back into the Great Plains during recent years.

While on the job of chasing tornadoes back into Mexico as soon as they appeared, Febold encountered a playful twister who wanted to wrestle. After a tough tussle, the Swede finally subdued the storm and tied it securely with a horsehair rope. Lying down to rest after his exertion, Febold soon dropped off to sleep. The tornado twisted out of the rope and skipped away, gleefully demolishing everything in sight before Febold awoke.

After cutting a path of destruction, the twister returned and attacked the sleeping man. First the storm bound the Swede with his own lariat. Then it whisked him to the top of a high hill, whirling through sand, water, and weather until Febold was completely encased in a cement-like mixture. Left on top of the hill with only his head sticking from the strange mixture, Febold waited nearly 72 hours before the horrified Indians finally found courage enough to approach the place and release him.

Needless to say, when the redskins asked him to resign his position of twister-stopper Febold announced that he had already quit.

Febold found that life was dull indeed without the excitement and adventure the twisters had provided.

It was a welcome diversion for him one afternoon when a big hail cloud hovered over the border. Dark as a stack of black cats at midnight, the foreboding cloud saw Febold then flicked forks of lightning from its lurid green lining, and sailed defiantly across the Mexican border. The cloud scattered a few stones to show Febold who was boss, then prepared to move majestically past him. The Swede grabbed one of the hail stones and threw it back with all his might. The cloud, completely taken by surprise, was punctured in a number of places. Hail ran from the holes and, as it happened, Febold was caught directly in line of the icy pellets. Completely inundated by the hail, the dazed Swede managed several hours later to dig himself from the pile of nature's ice cubes. In spite of his robust constitution, Febold caught a head cold and suffered with severe chillblains for several months afterward.

The Swede swore to give a wide berth to those green-lined clouds from there on in.

Febold was much bothered with mischievous tornadoes after he gave up his position as twister-stopper.

Every little breeze did its darnedest to destroy something on Febold's ranch. After rebuilding his ranch house for the fifteenth time, he decided that he must find a way to remedy the situation. He finally hit upon the idea of constructing his buildings on a series of springs and hinges so that when a storm cloud approached he could merely touch a button and the buildings would immediately lie flat on the ground. After the cloud passed, another touch of the button brought them back to their original shape. No damage was done, except possibly to furniture which had been in the way or otherwise interfered with the workings of the mechanism.

Febold found his invention highly successful. He was congratulating himself on his ingenuity after just outwitting a small whirlwind. Perhaps it was because he did not knock on wood, but later that afternoon the whirlwind returned with a large tornado. Febold pressed the button. The invention operated faithfully, but the big twister damaged one of the springs. After the storms had blown themselves out, the Swede pressed the button. Nothing happened.

It took six days and the entire tribe of the Dirtyleg Indians to clean up the mess.

CHAPTER THREE

REAL AMERICAN WEATHER

Somebody ought to do something about the weather. It's downright disgraceful that in most parts of the United States the climate is of foreign origin. Florida and California openly brag of their Mediterranean sunshine. Winter resorts in the Adirondacks advertise that they are authentic imitations of those in Switzerland. The only one place where one can get real, genuine American weather is on the Great Plains between the Mississippi and the Rockies. Of course, Nebraska's famous blizzard of 1888 blew in from Siberia.

In the early days it was even more American than it is now. At least that's what Febold's grand-nephew, Bergstrom Stromberg says. He's way past ninety and has seen some big weather in his day.

The Great Fog, old-timers believe, was the biggest piece of American weather that ever hit the Great Plains. It all began, Bergstrom Stromberg recalls, near the end of the Year of the Great Heat when it began to rain for the proverbial forty days and forty nights.

The rain, however, had no more chance of hitting the ground than a midget has of spitting into a blast furnace. The precipitation turned to steam which, when cooled a few minutes, turned into fog.

The milky mist was so thick that people had to go around in pairs, one to hold the fog apart while the other walked through it. The pioneer ranchers didn't have to water their stock. The animals simply drank fog. It must have looked funny to see pigs with their noses in the air rooting for fish and frogs, Bergstrom adds.

The dirt farmers, though, were as perturbed as the stockmen were happy. The sun couldn't shine through the fog, and the seeds, not knowing which was up, grew downward.

Things weren't too bad while the fog was more or less pliable, but after the freeze things were really done up white. For a time, the settlers tried to cut tunnels through, but this was exhausting if any great distance was to be covered.

Febold ordered English fogcutters, but they were slow in arriving so he built a stairway to the top of the fog, and travel was carried on up on top. When a person wanted to go somewhere he had to dig a hole down to the ground in order to find where he was. Trouble flared when numerous farmers staked out claims on top of the fog, directly over another's homestead. However, the settlers made the best of it. A number cut large rooms out of the fog and moved in, even papering the walls and hanging pictures.

Finally, because the English fogcutters were so slow in arriving, Febold himself tackled the job of ridding the state of the fog. He cut the misty moisture into long strips which he laid along the roads so as not to spoil the fields. In course of time, the dust covered the roads and today one can hardly tell where he buried the Great Fog. Many a rural mail-carrier, however, still curses Febold and his English fogcutters. Every spring when it rains or thaws, that old fog comes seeping up and makes rivers of mud out of all the country roads.

Take the popcorn ball, a typical American product. Most people think someone invented the popcorn ball, but it's actually a product of American weather. No, Febold did not originate the corn concoction; but the popcorn ball invented itself, so to speak, on his ranch near the Dismal River.

It was during that particular period known as the Year of the Striped Weather which came between the years of the Big Rain and the Great Heat. This year the weather was both hot and rainy. There was a mile strip of scorching sunshine, then a mile strip of rain. On Febold's farm were both kinds of weather.

The sun shone on his cornfield until the corn began to pop, while the rain washed the syrup out of his sugar cane. Now the canefield was on a hill and the cornfield was in a valley. The syrup flowed downhill into the popped corn and rolled it into a great ball.

Bergstrom Stromberg relates that some of the popcorn balls were hundreds of feet high and resembled gigantic tennis balls when seen from a distance.

40

One never sees any of them now because a great horde of grasshoppers devoured them one afternoon in July, 1874.

The Weather Bureau reported in a recent statement that Nebraska's winters were gradually becoming milder.

Bergstrom Stromberg recalls one winter in which there was no snow at all, according to a story told him by his great-uncle Febold. The ground had absorbed so much heat from the abnormally hot summer preceding that when snowflakes started to fall they melted and evaporated in midair.

Even the water flowing in the Platte was so hot that when Febold bucketed it out and carried it to his ranch to water his withering trees, it merely went "f-f-f-f-t!", formed steam and evaporated.

That winter, too, the ground was uncomfortably hot to walk on. Febold fitted the Dirtyleg Indians with mocassins which set a style for the redmen; soon all were wearing mocassins and the fad became a fixture with Indians forever after.

The Weather Bureau has never agreed whether or not Febold Feboldson was responsible for the cold wave which swept Nebraska one summer a number of years ago.

It seems that the summer had started off as a regular blowtorch affair. The peaks of the hills had melted down years before, but this summer melted them even more, and they soon refracted the sun's rays from surfaces as round as billiard balls.

One day the scorched settlers were chilled when a blast of cold air struck them from the north. The cold was so cold in contrast to the heat that a number of the settlers, as well as a score of Indians, were overcome by the change in temperature. Wave after wave of the cold air came down over the round-topped hills to the north, despite the sun which looked as hot as molten metal.

This kept up for the better part of a week, and all the people were wearing wool skirts and balbriggans, and laughing and singing as they worked in the fields. At night the sound of strange machinery in operation was borne southward on the cold waves.

One day, after a delightful morning, the air currents stopped. The extreme quiet that followed the cessation of the cold waves was broken by howls of dismay as the populace fought to get out of their heavy clothing. The sun beat down with ever-increasing force.

Seeking to find the reason for the cold waves as well as their sudden stopping, a party of settlers explored the north country. They found Febold sitting on a hill, gazing disconsolately at a tangled heap of machinery—copper tubing, cogwheels, gears, and pulleys. When the party asked Febold what was the matter, he gritted his teeth and a wild look came into his eyes. The frightened settlers did not remain for his answer.

And so the matter stands. Rumor has it that Febold had perfected the first mechanical refrigerator, which operated perfectly until some tiny flaw in its works resulted in its self-destruction.

CHAPTER FOUR

GREAT GUNS
AND LITTLE FISHHOOKS

To hear Bergstrom Stromberg tell it, fishing nowadays isn't what it used to be when he and his great-uncle Febold used to fish in the good old days.

Many a night the Swedish pioneer was kept awake by dogfish in the Dismal River barking at the moon. Methods of fishing, too, have changed considerably.

When Febold first came to the Great Plains, he found that the Dirtyleg Indians used tobacco for fish-bait. The redskins sat in their birchbark canoes and when the fish came up to spit, hit them in the head with their tomahawks. The Civil War stopped the tobacco supply and nearly ruined the fishing. Febold, however, came to the rescue with California raisins. Raisins did not make the fish spit but they put iron in their blood. The Dirtylegs then simply took them from the water with magnets.

Febold, one day, went fishing but when he arrived at his favorite spot on the Dismal River he discovered that he had forgotten the bait. He was about to return home when he noticed a snake slither through the weeds on the river bank; the reptile

44

was carrying a frog in his mouth. Febold offered to swap a drink of whiskey for the frog; the snake was willing and the trade was made.

The Swede baited up the hook, cast his line, and had not been fishing for more than ten minutes when he heard a great noise. It sounded like thunder mixed with the staccato clatter of castanets. He turned and his amazed glance fell upon a thousand rattlesnakes. Each wagged its tail like a contented pup; each held a frog in its mouth, eager for the swap.

Realizing that the half-pint bottle would never satisfy the snakes' thirst, Febold threw the bottle against the rock and broke it. The rattlers, hissing in unison like a locomotive letting off steam, glided toward the broken bottle, dropped their frogs and began to lap greedily at the amber liquor. So eager were the reptiles to quench their thirst that they failed to heed the glass splinters until their tongues were cleft. Snakes, to this very day, have forked tongues as a warning against voracity.

It has been explained how Febold became a temperate man; he was greatly opposed to the drinking of spirituous liquors by his Indian employees.

For his own personal enjoyment, however, he made a mild beverage of ragweed juice, thistlestems and buffalo berries, mixed with milkweed milk. He carried the liquid in a small flask and occasionally took a nip.

One day while fishing he had a chance to test the potency of his concoction. He had fished in a small creek for nearly three hours without a single nibble. When he pulled his line from the water he saw that the big fat worm with which he had baited his hook was nearly dead. Noting the discouraged look on the worm's face, Febold decided then and there that the worm, in its present condition, provided a pretty poor advertisement for the bright new hook he was using.

The Swede removed the worm, poured some of his special beverage down its throat, and put it back on the hook. He had no sooner tossed the line into the water than he felt a gigantic tug on the other end. Febold was hard put to keep from being pulled into the river. After a struggle, he was able to snub the line around a nearby tree; he gradually pulled it in until he had the fish on the bank.

It was a huge bass but what confounded Febold was the fact that the fish didn't even have the hook in its mouth. The worm had wrapped itself around the bass and held on with such determination that Febold finally had to cut the worm in two with his pocket-knife to get at the fish.

High water and big fishing remind Bergstrom Stromberg of how his great-uncle used to lasso sharks in the Platte River. That was back in the days when it really rained in these parts.

Every spring there was an annual flood, just as regular as taxes and the Sears-Roebuck catalog. The Platte would overflow its banks sometimes twenty feet or more so that everybody had to take to the hills. Sharks and whales would swim up from the Gulf of Mexico on a sort of spring vacation.

These floods were so regular that Febold thought he would make a little money fishing, because the marooned farmers were hard up for food. One year he caught some baby sea horses and fed them hair tonic. By the next season they were big enough to ride. Then Febold mounted a sea horse and galloped down the Platte, lassoing fish right and left.

Febold's fishing in the Platte came to an unforseen end. High water the next spring flooded the pens of his sea horses. The creatures escaped into the Gulf of Mexico and have never been seen this far north since.

Febold, aware of the popularity of dude ranches, attempted to convert his house on Dismal River into this type of accommodation for the tourist trade.

The Swede instituted a new system of fishing. He never allowed the use of lines or hooks. Because the Dismal River is thick with dogfish, Febold instructed the tourist fishermen to simply whistle. A whistle worked wonders; the dogfish clamored to leap into the whistler's boat. If Febold felt that someone was getting more than his share, he whistled under his breath and the dogfish cargo leaped back into the lake. Occasionally, a cunning fisherman would escape Febold's notice and his boat would be filled to almost overflowing; but that kind of person always whistled once too often and the fish sank the boat and escaped. Greediness was always punished.

Febold Feboldson, unlike Dan'l Boone and Kit Carson, did not stake his reputation upon his hunting prowess or his ability with a gun. One day, however, the Swedish plainsman had history-making luck.

Febold had taken his big six-gauge shotgun and gone hunting along the Platte for his winter's meat supply. His gun was a muzzle-loader fired by a huge hammer striking a cap; it was six feet seven inches long, weighed just 21 pounds, and the muzzle bore was the size of a half-dollar.

With only one cartridge left in the barrel, the Swede noticed a bear on the bank of the river. He forgot to remove the corn-cob from the end of the gun, which he used to keep it from getting dirty when he tramped around. Febold drew aim and fired. The gun exploded.

Parts of the barrel flew in all directions. Five geese overhead were killed by flying splinters. Splinters also accounted for a number of ducks swimming in the river. The explosion startled Febold and he jumped backwards, trampling a nest of pheasants to death. Turning to see what he had stepped on, the Swede lost his balance and fell into the river; his trousers acted as a seine and he caught nine catfish, a silver bass and two snapping turtles.

The corn cob from the gun barrel went through the bear and killed two owls sitting in an old dead tree. The bear fell against the tree and broke it off, disclosing a trunk full of honey. Some of the honey ran into the river and made the water so sweet that the remaining fish got the toothache and came to the surface. Febold easily caught them.

This story would have been told sooner; but Febold did not have a hunting license.

Febold made the first flight into the stratosphere—although he didn't exactly go himself. He was out walking one day when a bunch of geese flew over. Although he was without his gun, he wanted some of those geese mighty bad.

He picked up a rock to throw at the birds but in his eagerness squeezed the stone too hard, and it was crushed into a handful of sand. He found a small boulder which he threw at the flock with all his might. The geese were directly overhead, and Febold threw the stone so hard that it made a hole in the flock of geese, then kept right on going up. The boulder grew smaller and smaller, until it became a mere speck in the sky, then vanished completely. Febold watched, however, and saw it reappear. He managed to deftly catch it as it hurtled earthward.

In the first place, the boulder struck a goose, and carried it along on the trip. The bird was frozen solid, showing the temperature at the height the rock had reached. The fowl's eyes had glazed while it was at its greatest height, and in the dead eyes was a good picture of the earth below, one of the first photographic images showing the earth's curvature. The goose had "honked" several times, and these noises filtered down for several hours after the boulder had returned to the ground. And last of all, as Febold cooked the bird, he noticed several strange things which went "Zip-p-p!" and were out of sight before he could really get a good look at them.

Although they were great puzzles to Febold, Bergstrom Stromberg simply states that he is convinced they were atoms which had eluded the scientists.

Febold occasionally visited his nephews because he enjoyed their company on his hunting trips. One of his favorites on these expeditions was Hjalmar Hjalmarson who had a ranch on the Powder River.

One morning when Febold and Hjalmar were out hunting, the great-uncle took a pot shot at what he thought was a running coyote. It turned out to be the hat of a man who was riding down a small draw. It also turned out that the man was very angry. He told Febold to go for his gun as he aimed to get satisfaction.

Febold, always a peace-loving soul, didn't want any trouble but he realized that it would be useless to argue with the infuriated stranger. He drew his gun but, instead of shooting at the man, shot at the other's bullet. As the lead pellets met in midair they fell harmlessly to the ground midway between the two men. The man fired again and again at Febold, who cooly returned his fire, each time his bullet striking and stopping the other's bullet.

Amazed at this remarkable display of marksmanship, the stranger suddenly ceased firing, strode over to Febold, and stuck out his hand.

"I'm Pecos Bill," he introduced himself, "and I'm right proud to meet up with a gun-shooter nearly as good as I am."

That pile of lead still remains out there on the prairie; it may be rather hard to find now, but it's there, all right.

Buffalo Bill, known throughout the West as a crack shot, also met his match when he ran across Febold one afternoon.

Mr. Cody, armed with a fancy high-powered gun, had hunted in the hills all day and had nothing to show for it. He was surprised when he met the Swede carrying a small .22 rifle and a hunting bag filled with twelve rabbits and five geese. Buffalo Bill, astounded at such an exhibition of hunting prowess, began to praise Febold's ability to bring in such a catch with such a small weapon.

"Shucks, this here ain't nothin'," said the Swede. "Here comes Eldad Johnson with three buffalo, a b'ar, two wild cats and a Dirtyleg Indian."

"What weapon's he using?" asked Buffalo Bill.

"He took the sling shot," Febold told him.

Febold never claimed to be much of a runner but Bergstrom Stromberg declares that as sure as God made little green apples, if he had ever entered the Olympics the hardy Swede would have been way ahead and running easy.

Bergstrom recalls, for instance, that Febold was once far from home and had but one shell left in his gun. Plagued with a voracious appetite, the Swede decided to shoot the first animal he came across in order to appease his hunger.

Suddenly he saw a jack rabbit bob up out of his hole in the ground. Febold raised his rifle, took aim, and fired. Fearing that the rabbit might fall back down in the hole, Febold dropped his gun and ran toward the animal as fast as he could. He lunged forward and grabbed the rabbit by the ears—just as his bullet found its mark.

When Febold related this story to the Dirtyleg Indians, they looked at him with disbelief. Then they drew two fingers across their mouths. This Indian sign implied that the Swede had a forked tongue like a snake and that it was impossible to believe him.

Unhappy that he had been called a liar, Febold returned home and prepared for bed. Frequently before retiring, he blew out the light and jumped into bed before the room got dark. On this particular evening, not knowing that his trusty houseboy, Little Ptomaine, a retired Indian chief, had moved the furniture, Febold walked into the bedroom, blew out the light and jumped for the bed. Since the bed had been moved, the Swede struck the side of the house with such force that the foundation was stretched and the building tumbled into the basement.

Febold also had one of the most unique hideouts that anyone could imagine. He discovered it one day while hunting and resorted to using it only when hard pressed by attacking animals or hostile Indians. Hiding in this lair was a sure way to elude any pursuer.

The way Febold hit upon his hideout was novel. He was crossing the Platte River when he blundered into a quicksand and suddenly sunk from sight. Sure that he was doomed, the Swede was relieved to feel his feet strike something solid. Inves-

53

tigating, he found it was a covered wagon which had gone down at a previous time. Febold crawled into the wagon, buttoned up the flaps, and found it dry and comfortable inside.

He also found that by going out of the opposite end of the wagon, he could get back to the surface of the river without undue difficulty. To make the hideout practical, the Swede made a pipe of large-stemmed jointed snake-grass; he ran this pipe up from the wagon to a clump of willows near the south bank of the river. The snake-grass provided ventilation and furnished fresh air for limitless periods of time.

When harried, Febold would rush into the river, flounder elaborately in the quicksand, then disappear from sight. His pursuers, after watching him go under, were satisfied that he had drowned. They would ride away from the river, convinced that the Swede would never bother them again.

It is thought that Febold Feboldson was the only man to ever have a house at the bottom of the Platte River.

Febold was one of those humans plagued with the quick-growing variety of whiskers. The Swede didn't complain though; he just thanked his lucky stars and recalled the time that those whiskers saved his life.

One morning, immediately after Febold had finished shaving, an enemy Indian named Old Hot Shot, leading a band of warring braves, attacked the Swede at his ranch house on the Dismal River. He knew he didn't have a chance if he stayed inside so he bolted through the door, grabbed a fast horse from the corral and started away. Before he could say "Jack Robinson," Febold realized that the Indians had seen his escape.

Soon arrows whizzed all about the Swede. The redskins drew nearer and nearer. Febold could fairly feel his scalp tingle; Old Hot Shot had vowed to lift his hair and the unhappy Swede felt that his hour had come. The chase continued until they reached the Platte. Febold started his horse across, hoping to reach his special hiding place, the submerged covered wagon in the river bed.

The Indians, however, were too quick for him. Surrounded, Febold was dragged from his horse. Old Hot Shot raised his tomahawk and the Swede, seeing the bright blade glittering in the sun, began to say his prayers. Then the enemy Indian's arm stopped in midair. The redskin peered into Febold's face quizzically, then shrugged and dismissed his braves. The war party rode away.

Febold turned to the Platte and looked at his reflection in the river's surface. Then he understood. His fast-growing whiskers were almost six inches long; the dust his pony had kicked up had powdered them white. He looked like an old prospector and the enemy Indians had failed to recognize him.

This incident may have been the origin of the term "escaped by a hair."

CHAPTER FIVE

DROUTH BUSTIN'

The surest way to make an old-time plainsman sore is to remind him that geographers once labeled the Great Plains a part of the Great American Desert. When the talk comes around to this fact as a topic of conversation Bergstrom Stromberg has a great many uncomplimentary things to say about mapmakers. He will admit that there are few drouths now and then—but they are nothing compared to what they were when his great-uncle Febold was around.

According to Stromberg, Febold recorded volumes of facts regarding the driest year in all history. It was so dry that the ink dried, before it could set on the paper, and blew away, leaving the pages blank. Febold wasted several days chronicling the dry facts, only to find his efforts gone to naught.

That year was so dry that the few sprinkles that fell during the winter in the place of snow did nothing but start dust storms. Settlers gave up trying to raise crops after several lost good horses; the animals mired down in the dust and, unable to extricate themselves, suffocated. The Indians had to stay inside their wigwams during the daytime, because it was almost certain death to venture out into the sunlight. The redskins hunted and fished after sundown to keep from starving.

Febold stayed in his big log cabin on his ranch near the Dismal River, but the intense heat took all the moisture out of the logs. The structure shrank and warped until it became the only three-story dog house on the Great Plains. It got so dry that when a huge flood of water came down the Platte, it hit this section and disappeared in the sands, leaving no trace of any kind.

During this great drouth which devastated the crops of the early pioneers, Febold proved that it is not only "fun to be fooled"—but it's good business as well.

The Swede, that year, was ranging many hundred head of cattle. Since it did not rain, no grass grew on the flats where Febold's cattle usually grazed. Day by day in every way they got thinner and thinner. Febold tied sand bags on their tails because he feared that a heavy wind would blow his profits away.

Goaded to desperation, the cattleman thought and thought, but his usually resourceful mind failed to function. One evening, he sat in the lamplight at the table in his ranch-house, turning the pages of a mail-order catalog to distract his mind from its many disturbing thoughts. Suddenly he stopped! That was it! Right there—on this very page! Febold got pen and ink, wrote out an order, and in a few moments had it signed, sealed and ready for the Pony Express.

The package from the mail-order house finally came.

Settlers were amazed to see Febold's cattle grow fatter and fatter while their own stock dried up, dissipated completely, and blew away. Then an observant settler discovered the secret—Febold's cattle grazed contentedly among the cactus and thistles. Each cow was equipped with a pair of green glasses!

What the Plains country really needs, Bergstrom insists, is a good old drouth buster. Back in the early days, there was never a drouth ever came out of Kansas that Febold couldn't bust in 24 hours. Why, shucks, he was just too good at drouth-busting. When they heard about his phenomenal ability, the state of California hired him to stop their earthquakes. Bergstrom adds that there must have been some misunderstanding about salary or something because California seems to have quakes about as often as the Plains have drouths.

Febold was always a good-natured cuss, but he really got peeved one year when the weather got hotter and drier and drouthier every day. It spoiled his fishing. "This here sorta thing has gotta stop," Febold said to himself and began to think. He always was a fast thinker; in a few minutes he had thought of more than a hundred ways to bust a drouth.

At that time there were many lakes in the north hills, just as there are today. Times had gotten so bad that the settlers immersed themselves in the lakes several times daily to keep from drying up and blowing away.

Febold saw the solution to the problem. He built huge bon-fires around these lakes, and kept them burning for three weeks. In that length of time the water in the lakes got so warm it vaporized and formed clouds. These clouds bumped into each other trying to get away from the lakes, and this section of the country received bounteous rains. After once being primed, the regular rains came again, and the country was saved.

Was Febold considered a hero? No. The Indians then had no place in which to swim.

The Swede also found the "noise method" a highly satisfactory way to make rain. He recalled that it generally rained after battles, national conventions, and similar noisy affairs. But how to make enough noise? That was the problem. The Dirtyleg Indians were too lazy to cooperate; the white settlers were so dry they couldn't speak. Febold, however, wasn't a man easily stumped—not when he wanted to go fishing as badly as he did. He decided to enlist the aid of his fishing companions—the frogs who had good loud voices. But, Febold realized, a frog will not croak unless he's good and wet.

This difficulty was overcome in a minute. Febold hypnotized a couple of frogs and told them it was raining. They began to croak with joy to spread the news. Soon every frog in the country began to croak at the top of his voice. In a few minutes there was enough noise to give the Dirtyleg Indians' rain god a headache. According to specifications, the rain just poured down; everyone was happy, especially Febold and the frogs.

That was only one of the many ways to which Febold resorted to rid the parched Plains of drouth. It could only be used once a season, however, because so much rain fell that the frogs were washed clear down to the Gulf of Mexico. It took a whole year for them to get back, ready for Febold's next drouth-bustin' bout.

"I'm afraid this here noise method is too dern hard on the country," Febold admitted. "Next time I'll have to use somethin' a little gentler."

According to Bergstrom Stromberg, Febold's next plan was one of his best inventions because it was completely automatic. It not only turned on the rain, but it turned it off, too. The device, still working today as well as when Febold first tried it out, is timeless because it is based on human behavior. Human nature, you know, is always the same.

Ever since Febold first began to study the drouth problem, he noticed that people were always concerned about the weather. He observed that everybody kept saying "What a wonderful thing it would be if we'd only get a good rain." They ran to the thermometer, looked at the mercury and muttered, "Oh, dear, oh, dear!" Then they'd wipe their brows, look at the sky and start the whole procedure all over again.

Febold knew that a watched pot never boils. Of course, it wouldn't rain if people kept talking about rain. If people had to talk, let them talk about something else besides the weather.

The moment he grasped this idea, Febold knew he must find some way to distract people's minds. He must make them talk about something else. Now this wasn't as easy as it might sound.

Movies, baseball, automobiles, and radio stars had not yet been invented. People could talk about love, but they didn't. On moonlit nights, of course, they'd get out their git-tars and sing about love, but that didn't count. Febold decided to get people interested in his favorite indoor sport—the bull session.

Believe it or not, Bergstrom insists, it did the trick. Right in the middle of one of the worst drouths that had ever hit the Great Plains, Febold began to criticize the government. He lambasted every office-holder in the country from the county assessor to the secretary of the treasury. Gradually everybody began to realize that Febold had a very legitimate gripe. They joined the conversation, cussing and discussing the government. No mention of the weather was made for a whole 24 hours.

The inevitable happened. It began to rain and rained all night. In the morning, everyone said "My, what a fine rain! Just what we need!" The rain stopped then and there.

Nevertheless, Febold had introduced politics as a likely substitute for weather as a topic of conversation. The number and severity of drouths were reduced considerably. Of course, the system isn't foolproof. It doesn't work all the time, but during presidential election years you never saw such a wet country as the Great Plains.

Many believe that the irrigation ditches in western and central Nebraska are a modern feat of engineering. Old-timers scoff at their stupidity and recall Febold Feboldson's early attempts to inundate his fields during the dry years.

Febold, with the aid of his bull buffalo calf, Oscar, once pulled the Platte River from its bed and led it up over the hills to his ranch near the dried-up Dismal River. He proceeded to irrigate his potatoes with water from the misplaced Platte.

The Swede's sheep, also very dry, came up to drink from the river. As he sat watching them, Febold became very drowsy and was soon fast asleep. The next thing he knew, approximately eight feet of water covered everything and he was quite wet. One of the flash floods for which the Platte later became famous had struck with the sudden ferocity of a prairie rattler. The fact that Febold was the sole settler in that particular vicinity was the only thing that prevented a tremendous loss of life.

Learning by experience, Febold dragged the Platte back into place and hurriedly deepened a number of gulleys to drain off the excess flood water. The deepened gulleys eventually became rivers and proved helpful in preventing a repetition of a similar catastrophe at a later date. The three new rivers, Bergstrom points out, are the three branches of the Loup.

During another of the great drouth years, all the crops dried out except watermelons. They were plentiful all the way from the Mississippi River to Yellowstone Park. The hot water in the Yellowstone geysers gave Febold his great idea: He turned the geysers into the watermelon vines and shot the steam all over the country. He cleaned up a fortune selling the melons to the railroads to run their steam engines. Then, after they'd taken the steam out, he sold them again to the farmers for irrigation.

According to Bergstrom Stromberg, the system would be running today if Eldad Johnson's grandfather had not introduced corn mash into the vines. The revenue collectors got after

Febold for going into the whiskey business without a license. When Febold protested that he did not know what they were talking about, the officers declared that "ignorance of the law is no excuse." Febold was not prosecuted, but the revenue collectors destroyed his intricate irrigation system by disconnecting the watermelon vines from the Yellowstone geysers.

After the de-activation of his Watermelon Power and Irrigation Company Febold decided to drive a well from which he could irrigate in case the country had another drouth. Drouths, at that time, were as plentiful as flies around a jelly jar.

Febold hollowed out some tall, thin tree trunks for pipe and fastened a point of flint to the one he drove in the ground. As one was driven into the ground, he fastened another onto its end, and soon he had nearly twenty-five of these lengths buried in the ground. He had still not struck rock or sand.

The Swede, however, kept driving. Soon he felt a pain in his foot which increased each time he struck the pipe he was driving. He moved his foot to investigate, and found, in some manner, his tree-pipe had bent and after going so far had turned around and started up. Just then, water began to flow from both ends of the pipe. It is still flowing to this day.

When Febold, in his excitement, tried to tell an Indian about it, the warrior turned from him arrogantly and said "You are teasing me." Every time he tried to interest someone in his wonderful well, he would hear "Are teasing."

Later, other everflowing wells were made. Is it any wonder that they are called "Artesian"?

While many of Febold's shooting stunts are known, one of his greatest has only recently come to light, according to Bergstrom Stromberg.

The Swede had gained considerable prestige as a marksman and was darned proud of his reputation. However, the spring of 1887 was exceedingly dry and the irritable chief of the Dirtyleg Indians publically blamed Febold, saying he had displeased the God of Rain. Febold set out to compensate for the trouble he had caused the redskins.

He perched himself on a hill and waited until a black cloud came scudding across the sky, brimful of rain water but not spilling a drop. The Swede, after boring tiny round holes in the edges of the shells for his six-guns, shot at the cloud with both guns. The lead pellets struck the cloud and opened huge holes through which the water poured. Seeing the rain descending, Febold turned to receive the cheers of the awed Indians.

Again fate played a dirty trick on the Swede. A sudden change of weather brought colder temperatures and the rain froze in midair. Instead of raining it hailed. Febold's soft-nose bullets had torn such huge gaps in the cloud that the hailstones were as large as baseballs. The resulting storm was one of the most devastating in this part of the country.

Poor Febold, battered and bruised from the thumping given him by the hail, immediately started on one of his trips to California, realizing that he would be most unwelcome in the Dirty-leg Indian country until the unfortunate incident was forgotten.

CHAPTER SIX

THE DIRTYLEG INDIANS

The Dirtyleg Indians were not only one of the meanest tribes of heathens west of the Mississippi, but also one of the cleverest. Febold was cleverer than any redskin; at least, he must have been if one can believe Bergstrom Stromberg's story about duck hunting in the early days.

When Febold first settled in Nebraska, the Dirtylegs were still getting their ducks as their grandfathers had. They drove a herd of buffalo in a circle near the river until a large circular ditch had been made by the pounding hooves. When the Indians saw a flock of ducks about to alight on the river, they turned the river water into the ditch. The ducks followed the water round and round until they became dizzy and dropped to the ground. The Dirtylegs sprang from their hiding places, picked up the ducks and wrung their necks.

During the Year of the Great Heat the rivers were dry; only the shallow hill ponds contained water. Since the Dirtylegs could not make the few inches of water in these ponds flow in a desired direction, Chief Tummihake sent a delegation to Febold to appeal for help.

"Wal, you Injuns have always been gosh-awful braggarts," Febold observed casually, "You oughta have big enough lungs to catch a few ducks. I gotta idea. Come along."

Febold, Tummihake and the Dirtyleg delegation departed for the sandhills. The Swede stationed the Indians in the underbrush which circled one of the ponds. Just as a flock of ducks was about to light on the pond, Febold yelled "Blow!" The Indians blew the water away and the ducks stuck feetfirst in the mud.

Under Febold's direction, the Indians dug tunnels under the pond and built fires there. The ducks were roasted without being touched by human hands.

To show his gratitude to Febold for preventing his tribesmen from perishing of starvation, Chief Tummihake made him an honorary member of the Dirtyleg tribe. The Swede's honorary Indian name was especially appropriate; translated into English, the name means Old-Stick-in-the-Mud.

The name of the Dirtyleg tribe had an interesting origin, according to Bergstrom Stromberg who relays the story his great-uncle Febold Feboldson had told.

The tribe, originally, was a branch of the Blackfoot nation; historians since have never quite distinguished between the two. The Dirtylegs, however, were a separate division, although they were always somewhat weaker than the Blackfeet. A very popular brave of the Blackfeet tribe was Dirty Look; it was he who led the uprising against Chief Broken Arch. The rebellion was squelched and Dirty Look was banished from the tribe.

So great was his popularity that many of the Blackfeet followed him into exile. Dirty Look was voted chief and, as the banished tribesmen were denied horses, they tramped through the burned country that had been swept by prairie fires. They settled in the country along the Platte River. Other Indians made fun of the walking party and kept reminding them of their "dirty legs."

It was not from this fact, however, that they derived their name, but from the name of their chief, Dirty Look. The tribe was referred to as "Dirty Look's Tribe."

Among other things for which Febold and the Dirtyleg tribe are responsible is the expression "stung by the presidential bee." The term evolved from an actual incident.

Febold raised bees on his ranch near the Dismal River; their entomological antecedents drew the plow which made the Kansas-Nebraska boundary line. Standing Pat, a no-account buck of the Dirtyleg tribe, attempted to steal a bee one day. He had carefully picked up the bee by its wings but the insect flitted from his fingers and stung him painfully. Shrieking with anguish, the Indian was soon swollen to twice his natural size. Attracted by his cries, the Dirtylegs came running from all directions. They were amazed at his gigantic stature and made him chief of the tribe on the spot.

68

His mind operating with its accustomed sagacity, Febold instantly detected the possibilities in the sale of "chief bees," as the Indians termed his insects. The Swede began to peddle them to the redskins, allowing one bee to be sold to the highest bidder in each tribe. When the United States Government took charge of the Indian lands and put all the tribes on reservations, Febold's lucrative racket was put out of operation.

His bees brought good prices, however, when Febold sold them to Tammany Hall and Wall Street. Instead of chief bees, however, they became known as "presidential bees."

Bergstrom Stromberg recalls that Febold always regretted the transaction because of the unethical way the New York politicians handled these bees. Instead of stinging one man and letting him be president, they stung a dozen and let them fight it out. "—And the bad part of it is," summarized Bergstrom, "the man who loses always gets stung the worst."

About the time early settlers were trading rifles to the Indians for furs, Febold decided to get his share of the profits. The Indians, happy to replace their out-of-date bows and arrows with a more effective weapon, found that Febold could supply their need for hunting accessories.

The Swede hunted buffalo by night. From their horns, he fashioned powder horns which he traded to the Indians by day. A swappin' fool from way back, Febold bartered the horns for wild animals which the Indians snared and trapped.

Soon Febold was known throughout the entire Indian empire

as "Trader Horn." The name in Dirtyleg dialect was originally "Trade-Her-A-Powder-Horn," but this was soon shortened to the easier-to-say and more convenient "Trader Horn."

Febold, as a result of his bartering, soon acquired a large variety of wild animals. After erecting a huge tent made of buffalo skins, the Swede exhibited these beasts to the Indians. For admission, he charged so many powder horns; thus he had a self-sustaining business.

One time Febold stopped at an Indian village and a chief asked him to share his wigwam.

The chief and Febold sat up most of the night, swapping stories in Indian sign language. Along toward morning, after each of his fanciful tales was topped by a bigger and better one, Febold gave up and went to sleep.

In the morning, after he had saddled up his horse and was ready to depart, Febold realized that he had neglected the formality of introducing himself to the Indian chief, who had offered his hospitality.

"I should have done this before," Febold apologized, holding out his hand. "I'm Febold Feboldson."

As the old Indian took his hand and spoke, Febold realized why he had failed to outyarn him.

"Ugh!" the chief grunted. "Me big Chief Sitting Bull."

Febold Feboldson had one of the most stentorian voices in the history of the state. His father had been a town crier in his little village in Sweden and Febold proved himself a chip off the old block.

One day he found a horse and, since he could find no claimants, offered to sell the stray animal. He shouted the news to a nearby Indian camp. The sound of his voice was so great that it carried into the next valley. These Indians also came to see what caused the excitement. Encouraged, Febold shouted louder than before.

In a few moments, he had attracted a huge crowd of redskins. He proceeded to state the facts regarding the animal for sale, then sold him to the Indian who offered him the most.

Later, the Indians, when they had anything for sale, would look up Febold and use his voice to enable them to gather a crowd. This practice has become a modern art today; each town has its criers or, as we call them, auctioneers.

One of the first, if not the very first, elections ever held west of the Mississippi river was the election which Febold instituted when the tribes of both the Dirtyleg and Blackfeet Indians were without chiefs.

About to engage in the usual civil war which had always preceded the election of a new chief, the Indians were hesitant when Febold, using a little old-world diplomacy, talked them into holding a regular election. Each tribe put up candidates who campaigned vigorously until the election day arrived.

Febold, bitten by the campaign bug and always eager for public acclaim, joined the candidates and soon had his stump speeches going strong. This took the Indians by surprise; they had never heard of anything like this little shenanigan Febold was pulling. The Swede high-pressured the vote-casting Indians to such an extent that his name was written on all the ballots by the confused redskins.

When the ballots were counted and the sums totaled, Febold Feboldson was declared the new chief of the Dirtyleg and Blackfeet Indian tribes!

Since the tribes were hereditary enemies, the thought of being united under one chief disturbed them greatly. This meant no more wars—no more scalping—no more tomahawks or bows and arrows! When they recalled how Febold's duplicity had tricked them, both tribes decided there was only one way to deal with the Swedish deceiver—burn him at the stake to celebrate Election Day.

Febold, however, filled with the pioneer plainsman's saving intuition, anticipated danger. When the Indian avengers arrived they found a note pinned on the door of Febold's ranch house near Dismal River; it informed them that Febold had been called to California on one of his periodic business trips.

Febold Feboldson added his name to the long list of many other early settlers who owed their lives to the repeating rifle.

The Swede had just purchased a number of these new guns when the Dirtyleg Indians declared war and surrounded his ranch on the Dismal River. Febold clamped the guns at every window of the house and tied a string from the trigger of each rifle to a huge bull frog. The frog, attempting to escape, jumped in every direction; each jump discharged two or three of the rifles. Because of the superior aiming which Febold had done, each crack of a rifle spelled the doom of several Indians.

The redskins, thinking that the United States cavalry had arrived, made a panic-stricken departure for the hills. Febold's idea was the inspiration of the modern machine gun.

Out on a hunting expedition, Febold Feboldson was once cornered by a roving band of Dirtyleg Indians. He kept them at bay as long as his ammunition held out, but soon was horrified to see that he was out of lead balls, although he had plenty of powder. Hurriedly he rolled up mud balls, put them in his gun, and waiting until the Dirtylegs were very close, shot them, being careful to hit each Indian in the face where the mud would be most effective.

Following the battle, after Febold had dispatched the band, a government wagon train came along and helped him bury the defunct redskins. The medical men in the train noticed that each Indian had a mouthful of mud; in their clinical report to the government, the medical officers indicated that death was undoubtedly due to the fact that the Indians had "bitten the dust." That was the origin of the often-used phrase, "to bite the dust."

CHAPTER SEVEN

SNAKES ALIVE AND OTHER PETS

Febold Feboldson was fond of pets.

He brought dogs, cats and squirrels with him from back East when he came to Nebraska to settle. The cats, however, did not like their new home and howled constantly. The noise got on Febold's nerves so much that he experienced one of his ferocious fits of temper. He caught his cats and chopped off their tails. This enraged the felines and they went wild. The descendants of these cats, in fact, were later called Wild Cats or Bob Cats. And what became of the tails which Febold had chopped off? He threw them away and they took root along little creeks of the Great Plains. They are known today as "cat tails."

Febold did not attempt to domesticate the squirrels. He turned the animals loose but the befuddled creatures were lost on the treeless prairies. One day the Swede discovered that all his squirrels had disappeared. He was sure that the unhappy animals had either died of homesickness or had been devoured by coyotes.

About a week later, however, the squirrels returned. They were footsore and weary but the cheeks of each were puffed with nuts and seeds. They dropped their loot near Febold's home and again disappeared. The Swede's curiosity got the better of him and he followed the squirrels; he found that the animals traveled clear to the Missouri River where there were trees. There they picked up nuts and seeds from the trees and returned to Febold's ranch.

Today, the groves planted by Febold's squirrels provide shade and verdant beauty along many of the rivers of the Great Plains.

One day, while taking a walk along the banks of the Platte River, Febold came upon a common house cat caught in a crude Indian trap which had been set to snare water animals. The cat's leg was so badly injured that amputation was necessary to save the animal's life. When he saw the difficulty the feline had in getting around, Febold whittled a wooden leg from a hickory stick.

He strapped this on the animal and, after considerable practice, she soon became quite proficient in the use of her hickory member. Being a well brought-up cat, she was very grateful to Febold; she followed him about constantly and did many things to repay him for his kindness.

But the thing that topped them all, according to Bergstrom Stromberg who heard Febold himself relate the story, was an odd incident which occurred one night at Febold's ranch on the Dismal River. Hearing a strange noise, the Swede got out of bed, tiptoed to the door and peeked into the next room. A shaft of moonlight lighted the cat who sat beside a rat hole with her wooden leg poised in the air. Each time a rodent appeared through the hole, the cat knocked it over the head with her wooden leg. Every now and then the cat, looking behind at the growing pile of rats, smiled with pardonable pride.

Febold once tried to domesticate mugwumps; once plentiful in the Great Plains when the Swede first settled in the area, the species is now extinct.

He began an extensive project of mugwump farming, hoping that he could teach the Indians to eat mugwumps instead of prairie chickens and sage hens. Febold suffered a severe financial setback with this plan, one of the few unsuccessful ventures in which he was involved.

One day he forgot to feed the mugwumps their daily ration of ground-up woodpecker holes. The birds, known for their ravenous appetites, ate the holes from around the nails during the night. Naturally, the nails fell out and the house collapsed on the mugwumps, killing every last one.

Left with a large number of woodpeckers which he had kept to supply the mugwumps with holes, Febold fed and fattened the birds. Then he killed them, pickled them and sold them to fishermen for bobbers.

Speaking of animals, Febold had a most unusual pet—a rattle-snake who was as big around as a man's leg. The Swede called her Arabella. She grew to a length of fourteen feet, and when she rattled it sounded like a colored convention around a dice box. And she was gentle—she'd eat off your hand.

Bergstrom Stromberg well remembers Arabella. She was very friendly toward Febold's friends, and sought to pay them attentions which were not always welcome. Bergstrom declared the dern snake once chased him fully three-quarters of a mile before she caught up with him and caressed him with a playful squeeze of her coils. Bergstrom thought he was a goner for sure, but Febold laughed so hard that he dislocated one of his ribs.

Every morning at six o'clock Arabella crawled into Febold's bedroom and wagged her tail. The ensuing racket aroused the Swede from his slumbers. Nor would Arabella cease her rattling until Febold was wide awake or so angry he could no longer sleep.

Several times the snake proved to be a nuisance. Once, when a Russian noble was visiting Febold's ranch on the Dismal River, the Swede forgot to warn him about the reptile. Right on schedule, Arabella went in and rattled. The noise was soon matched by the clatter of the nobleman's knees; then, recovering his strength, he dashed through a window and disappeared down the road, never to be seen again in these parts.

Another time, Febold praised his foresight in befriending Arabella. A group of marauding Cheyennes had made an early morning raid and captured the settler. They were in the act of burning him at the bedpost when Arabella slithered into his room to rattle him up. Finding him not in his bed, the snake circled the room and saw Febold trussed to the bedpost. Arabella approached and the Indians, seeing the rattler headed straight for the white man, decided that death by snakebite would be more torturous than death by fire. They retired to watch Febold's agony.

Arabella came up to Febold, rubbed her head lovingly against his leg, and circled the bed to see what was the matter. She squirted venom on his thongs and the ropes disintegrated, releasing Febold. The Swede and his pet quickly cleaned the ranchhouse of marauding Indians.

One day Febold and Arabella went for a stroll, and the snake was rattling a little ditty as she writhed along. Febold was humming an accompaniment. Bergstrom Stromberg, who recalls this tale, surmised that the tune was the national anthem of all rattlesnakes. At any rate, all the rattlers in the country were soon gliding along behind Febold and Arabella, listening to the music.

The first thing Febold knew he was surrounded by rattlers, the writhing mass stretching as far as the eye could see. Escape was impossible!

His jaw dropped and naturally the humming stopped. Immediately there arose a fearful clamor as the snakes rattled their anger at his stopping the music.

Arabella offered a practical solution to the situation. She rattled a few bars of Brahm's "Lullabye," and soon the snakes were fast asleep. Febold and Arabella made a hasty exit, but it was weeks before Febold could look at the rattler without misgivings.

The Swede and his unique pet often rode horseback through the snake country after their encounter with the rattlers. Febold made a special basket on the back of his saddle just for Arabella.

She rode with him there, contentedly rattling. In fact, a seat behind a saddle soon became known as a rattle-seat. The term, however, has been corrupted through the years and has become "rumble seat" to designate the back seat of an automobile.

Bergstrom Stromberg expresses grave concern over the number of cacti which sprang up in Nebraska during the dry years. He says he hopes the plant will not get a start like it once had in the state. When one declares he had never heard that the cactus had been over-abundant in Nebraska, Bergstrom just naturally hits the roof.

"What!" he bellows. "You never heard of the Cactus Massacre? Why, that is one o' the highlights o' history in this neck o' the woods!"

The Cactus Massacre was preceded by one of those years of extreme drouth. The next year, when the rains came, there was nothing for them to help; everything had burned down to the sands except a species of drouth-resistant cactus. Refreshed by the abundant rains, this plant began to grow profusely. The fertile soil and lack of competition acted as a stimulus. Soon cactus was everywhere—and still growing.

A detachment of United States Cavalry, out after marauding Indians, camped one night in a clearing in the cactus. The fast-growing stuff closed in on them during the night, and by morning the detachment was completely wiped out; each man and his horse had died a horrible death—pierced through with thousands of spiny spears.

This was the Cactus Massacre. The government immediately took up the fight to reclaim Nebraska from cactus. The resulting war was one of the greatest in the history of the country. The government, after several losing encounters with the rapidly growing scourge, enlisted the aid of Febold Feboldson and his indomitable pet rattle snake. With his fourteen-foot pet at his side, Febold experimented but found no practical means of stopping the cacti onrush.

He finally discovered that a spray made of rattlesnake venom caused the cacti to wither and die. With Arabella furnishing the poison and Febold distributing it with a special spray-gun of his own invention, the tide of victory finally turned toward Febold and the United States Government.

Arabella, however, who had been giving until it hurt, finally just rolled over and turned up her toes. To console the heart-broken Febold, the government gave the gallant rattlesnake a funeral with full military honors.

CHAPTER EIGHT

THE COYOTE CURE

Not the least of Febold's exploits and public benefactions was his saving of the old cattle kingdom when it was threatened with extinction by the mournful coyotes.

In the early days, according to Bergstrom Stromberg, the ranges were infested with packs of coyotes which set up such mournful wails that the cattle became dejected and melancholy. In this condition, they went about for days, never touching food or water. The mournful cries of the coyotes were slowly starving them to death.

At first the ranchers organized hunting parties and went out to round up and shoot the beasts. Whenever the hunters came upon the coyotes, however, the animals bayed so mournfully that not even Febold, undoubtedly the toughest hombre of the lot, had the heart to pull a trigger. Bergstrom believes that the animals were so depressing that they were the forerunners of the depression which devastated the nation's economic system after the Wall Street crash of 1929.

The cattlemen, after the coyote hunts failed, sat around watching their dogies die. But not Febold! No, sir, that Swede was thinking fast and furious—trying to hit upon a practical idea for ridding the range of this scourge. He thought of a thousand and six schemes, but discarded them all untried. His thousand and seventh scheme, however, he considered practical. At any rate, he decided to give it a try.

"What this country needs," Febold said, thinking aloud, "is an animal more dismal than the coyote. We must find some beast that will depress the coyotes as they are depressing the cattle. Sa-a-ay, wait a minute! I think I've got it! I know where I can get just such a critter. I'll write to my old friend Paul Bunyan and have him send me some of them there dismal saugers. Paul says them's the mournfullest animals that be."

The Swede sent to the north woods for a shipment of dismal saugers. This beast is one of those animals one reads about. He doesn't make a sound himself but lumbermen have been known to go stark, staring mad after they have met the dismal sauger in a swampy forest. The drip-drip-drip of the dank marsh water from the beast's beard does the trick.

In a few days, Paul Bunyan sent Febold the following message by his carrier bumble bee:

"You crazy old Swede:

"You ought to know that the dismal sauger is a swamp and forest animal. He would be unable to live on the lone prairie. Instead, I am sending a hundred gross of whimpering whing-dings. They ought to do the job.

X—P. Bunyan (his mark)."

83

They did the job all right. In two days all the wailing coyotes between the Mississippi and the Rocky Mountains had crawled off and died of sheer, inconsolable grief.

No one except a drunkard ever sees a whingding anymore, because the unhappy animals got to whimpering on each others' shoulders and finally cried themselves to death.

The whingding was one of the many early American animals which inhabited the Great Plains. Oodles of them existed here before Febold, intrepid hunter and trapper that he was, captured them all for the sanitarium of Doctor Keeley, the founder of the famous Keeley cure for *delirium tremens*.

Before Febold's expedition, Doctor Keeley had been able to deal only with those animals which resulted from drinking imported European beverages. These animals—the griffin, chimera, unicorn and gargoyle—were elements of old-world tradition; devices for capturing and combating them when they manifested themselves to unfortunates who had imbibed too freely, had been developed through the centuries.

Everything had gone satisfactorily for Doc Keeley until his patients began to know an insatiable thirst for American-made beverages. The most popular was corn whiskey which was the chief drink of the corn-growing states of the Great Plains. The doctor, then, began to encounter giddyfish, ding-toed awks, lopsided awgers, hodags, and suchlike American critters. At first he experimented with the griffin cure upon a patient who complained that he was constantly followed by a hodag; the beast,

84

wearing a pink-and-purple polka-dotted bow tie, refused to be routed.

"I must find a cure for corn," announced Doctor Keeley in a banner headline, after giving the newspapers an exclusive personal interview.

The newspaper account continued with Keeley's assumption that he could effect the cure he sought if only he could isolate and capture species of the American critters which haunted the deliriums of his patients.

"Leave that to me," Febold promised. "Down in my neck o' the woods—I mean plains—we gotta million of 'em."

Febold returned to the Plains and captured all the hodags, awks, and other such critters. He sent these to Doctor Keeley for experimentation. In return for this favor, the distinguished physician cured Eldad Johnson's grandfather who had degenerated into a chronic alcoholic. After a brief stay at the Keeley sanitarium, the old man returned to his home near Febold's ranch on the Dismal River. The cure had effected a miraculous transformation. Eldad was bright-eyed, firm-footed and his cherry nose, which once glowed like a Mack truck's tail light in the dark, now looked like a burnt-out light bulb.

One day while crossing the prairie, Febold congratulated himself that the air was no longer rent by the wailing coyotes and the whimpering whingdings. Suddenly he stopped and sniffed the air. His keen nostrils detected the unmistakeable smell of burning grass. Immediately a chill of apprehension passed over him for he was well aware of the danger of prairie fires.

He started at top speed for his ranch house, but had not gone far when the horizon to the northwest grew hazy and a puff of wind foretold a freshening breeze that would soon fan the flames to express-train speed.

In despair, he stopped, not knowing which way to turn. Turning, he dashed to the Dismal River and whistled for his dog-ducks. These faithful fowls flocked to him, each shaking water from its shaggy feathers. Febold, reverting to duck talk—something like pigeon-English—hurriedly explained the situation. With a chorus of loud quacks, the dog-ducks showed their knowledge of the need for speed. Each duck sprang into the river, immersed itself, and took wing for the northwest. Arriving over the fire, the ducks shook themselves as wet dogs do; it was from this unusual characteristic that the creatures derived their name. The ducks made several flights before the flames were extinguished.

Once more Febold had saved the country for his progeny—or, at least, for someone else's.

CHAPTER NINE

THE MOST INVENTINGEST MAN

Although the history books have never given him credit, the inventingest man to hit this country was Febold Feboldson. According to Bergstrom Stromberg, his famous great-uncle taught Eli Whitney, Robert Fulton, Alexander Graham Bell, Luther Burbank and Thomas Edison all they knew about inventing—and still had thousands of ideas left over.

Why, Febold could even invent animals. In the Year of the Many Rains, for instance, the weather was so wet that all the chickens in the country were dying of starvation. Their feet just sank into the mud and they mired down, unable to get out and forage eats.

The situation was, to say the least, becoming desperate, but as usual, Febold came to the rescue. He put webbed feet on the chickens, then flattened their bills so that they would be better adapted to probe water or mud while looking for grub. Unthinkingly, the great Swede had invented a new species of fowl. They took to the water and were so satisfied with their new equipment that they would not allow it to be taken off. They even tried to swim and the Indians, amused at the way the fowl kept tipping and going under the water, called them ducks.

Febold was a great person to fret over lost energy. He even worried about his dogs and the energy they wasted by turning around three times before lying down. Little things like that kept him thinking. Febold realized, of course, that this was a hangover from the days when dogs were wild and ranged in country covered with tall grass; the untamed canines had to turn around several times to flatten the grass before they could lie down.

The Swede devised a scheme to utilize this wasted energy. He made soft beds for the dogs on circular treadmills, then told the dogs long-winded stories of his experiences. Although they were accustomed to leading a dog's life, the animals found that Febold's highly colored accounts, entertaining at first, soon became repetitious re-hashes of tales told over and over again. This made the dogs sleepy—which was just what Febold expected. When they started to lie down, they turned around several times; this started the treadmill which, in turn, started the windmill which pumped water for Febold's stock.

Just as the dogs were ready to lie down, the Swede would shout "Sic 'em!" The dogs woke up immediately and Febold continued his story. The procedure proved satisfactory for a while and provided plenty of water in the tanks during the dry weather.

One night, however, Febold started for bed. He was quite sleepy but on his way upstairs he got to thinking. After three hours, he suddenly discovered that he was not on the stairs at all but had inadvertently stepped onto one of the treadmills. He rushed to the tank to see what had become of all the water he had pumped. To his dismay, he discovered that the water had run into a small hole in the ground, then back into the well. The same water had been used over and over again.

Appalled at this atrocious waste of energy Febold pulled up the well and threw it away—leaving the water standing there.

Once while passing through a swamp along the south side of the Dismal River, Febold attempted to light his pipe and caused a terrific explosion. After much investigation, the Swede determined the cause: a kind of marsh gas, escaping upward from the swamp, was highly inflammable.

"Why not utilize the gas for heating purposes?" queried Febold.

He hurried home, gathered up all the buffalo robes he could find, sewed them together and made a huge cover for the swamp. With the help of his pet gopher, Lizzie, he dug tiny tunnels from the swamp to the various tepees in the Dirtyleg Indian village. The gas was then piped from the marsh to the redskins' wigwams. A little gas was lost by outside competition when curious moles tried to hook on to the gas line, but the loss was slight.

Febold even went so far as to freeze a number of gopher holes during one winter, then dug them up and laid them across the ice on the Dismal River to supply a suburb of the Dirtyleg village on the north bank. With the first thaw, however, the pipe melted and the Swede decided that the iced gopher holes were not at all practical.

The gas business came to an unfortunate end. Dirtyleg Indians, indignant and angry, surrounded the Swede's ranch house, demanding that he remove their gas fittings. When the redskins had quieted enough to tell Febold what had motivated their sudden change of mind, he learned that an inquisitive skunk had lost his way under the hood cover of the swamp.

When the Union Pacific railroad was being built, the engineers came to Febold and asked his advice on how far west the road should run.

"Clean to Shanghai," Febold advised them.

"We'll build the road as far as Los Angeles if you'll build it the rest of the way," the railroad men compromised.

To hold up his end of the bargain, Febold continued the road from the California city to Shanghai. He used his famous balloon-caterpillar track. Each engine and coach was inside its own oval track like a war tank is inside its moving tread. The tracks were made of hard rubber attached to inflated rubber tires. As each car went over the water it laid down its own tracks in front of it and took them up behind.

The first train got as far as the Hawaiian Islands; they were known as the Sandwich Islands in those days. Eldad Johnson's grandfather, who was engineer on the trip, stopped for a snack. When his back was turned the train ran away. To his dying day Eldad declared somebody shanghaied it.

Bergstrom Stromberg is firmly convinced that the train is still in operation on the ocean floor and may be responsible for earthquakes, water spouts, and tidal waves.

Most people would be surprised to learn that the strings of colored lights which decorate modern Christmas trees are not a recent invention. Bergstrom Stromberg well remembers the holiday decorations which his great-uncle used on his ranch near the Dismal River.

Throughout the summer Febold hoarded lightning bugs and glowworms. About the middle of December, the bugs, petted and pampered, had grown very fat. He strung them on large strings and suspended them between his three-story ranch house and other buildings.

Deciding that there was not enough contrast between the glowworms and the fireflies, the Swede painted the worms red and the bugs green, so he could tell which was which at night. If one of the bugs or worms froze and went out, he quickly replaced it with a new bug or worm, whichever the case might be.

The lightning bugs did not give a steady light, and their flickering on and off, off and on, undoubtedly inspired the inventor of the modern traffic light, Bergstrom implies.

The guy who wrote "A Bicycle Built for Two" would be amazed to learn that he has made the velocipede more famous than the man who invented it: Febold Feboldson.

During one of the many particularly dry years, the Swede's horses ate cactus thinking it was prairie grass. Horribly indisposed, the animals were unfit for service. For months afterwards cactus spines worked out of the animals' innards, sometimes through their backs. One barb penetrated the saddle and Febold was unable to sit comfortably for several weeks.

He did not use his horses for riding after this attack. Growing exceedingly tired of walking in the months that followed, the Swede suddenly got a bright idea, the one which evolved into the first bicycle.

Febold caught a pair of hoop snakes, gave them a shot of moonshine whiskey and made them put their tails in their mouths. When the hooch took effect, the snakes became petrified, forming perfect circles; they became the first bicycle tires. He had the contraption arranged so that he could sit on a small seat, guide the front wheel, and propel himself forward by pushing with his feet on the ground. This invention proved highly satisfactory and Febold used it until his horses were again serviceable.

The Swede might have used his new means of transportation until the day he left the Great Plains if the Dirtyleg Indians had not been so openly contemptuous.

"Huh! White man heap big fool," the redskins pointed. "Him sit down and walk!"

One of the most controversial issues in the history of war is the booby trap. Experts are still undetermined as to how this destructive device originated. They should realize that only a mind like that of the mighty Febold Feboldson possessed the cunning and imaginative genius to devise the booby trap.

It all began when the mighty Swede became aware of the midnight raids certain unscrupulous Dirtyleg Indians made on his watermelon patch. He had bought the seed in Georgia and planted most of his ranch in melons. Although it was a dry year,

93

Febold found that the mournful whingdings were still around; he utilized the curious creatures in his irrigation plans. He staked the whingdings near his potato patch. Their wailings made the eyes of the spuds water like a Platte River flash flood. Febold, with typical foresight, had planted the potatoes parallel to the melons. The water provided irrigation for the melons until the whingdings, encouraged to cry, pined away completely and eventually disappeared. The Swede then resorted to onions planted parallel to the potato patch to furnish moisture for his watermelons.

Of course, the crop prospered, and the depredations of the Dirtylegs were Febold's sole worry. His imaginative mind did not puzzle long over the matter, however. He hollowed out every fourth melon, inserted a rattlesnake, and replaced the plug.

For several weeks thereafter when the Indians stole a melon, they often found a huge rattler on their hands. Febold, calculating the money he expected from his crop, discovered that he had forgotten which melons contained rattlers. Knowing that his crop could never satisfy the specifications of the Pure Food and Drug Act, the Swede gave away his entire crop.

Since the original seed had come from Georgia, and many of the melons contained actual rattlers, it is thought that Febold's fling at the watermelon industry, besides introducing the booby trap, also originated the now-famous Georgia Rattlesnake Watermelon.

Febold Feboldson loved nothing more than a battle of wits. Because of this, he gambled; not to win but to match wits with his opponents.

One of the most impossible wagers ever made, and one which old-timers still discuss, was Febold's bet with John Cody, a neighboring settler.

The wager, made on the spur of the moment, was fantastic; it was no wonder that Cody took him up immediately. The Swede wagered fifty head of horses that he could raise a crop, to be chosen by himself, without touching it or allowing anyone else to touch it. The wager also stipulated that the crop was to be harvested and stored in a building on Febold's Dismal River ranch—untouched by human hands. It sounded like a sure thing to Cody who failed to consider the resourcefulness for which the Swedish plainsman was noted.

Febold chose watermelons as his crop. He planted them on a hillside near his ranch. He spent many nights sitting up in his patch, his rifle across his knees, to keep hungry redskins from the ripening watermelons. When it hailed, Febold held umbrellas over his crop.

At last his labors were rewarded. The melons were ripe, rich red and honey-sweet. How to get them into the crib was another matter. Then, the evening that Febold discovered his crop was ready for harvesting, the first freeze of the fall occurred. The melons were nipped loose from their vines and started rolling downhill. Febold opened the door of his barn and the melons obligingly wobbled in.

Undoubtedly, this is the origin of the expression "hitting the broad side of a barn."

Needless to say, Febold won his wager and John Cody, who was the grandfather of Buffalo Bill, swore he'd never bet again with a rascal like Febold Feboldson.

Whenever corn-shucking time rolls around, Bergstrom Stromberg recalls the contest between his great-uncle and Swan Swanson, an obscure ancestor of Stromberg himself on his mother's side.

A shot was fired to start the contest. Febold was driving a pair of Jack Rabbit mules (in those days jack rabbits grew to be nearly as large as mules do nowadays) and was soon in the lead, with Swanson close behind. Febold husked faster and faster, one ear after another flying against the bang-board and into the wagon box. The box began to get warm—and warmer—until the corn began to pop. The popped corn soon filled the wagon and ran out onto the ground. Febold's mules saw the popcorn and, thinking it was snow, began to shiver and shake like a tent-show dancer at the county fair. Soon they were so cold they froze to death! Swanson's team, close behind, also saw the popcorn snow, and dropped dead in their tracks. Febold was adjudged the winner, since he had been in the lead.

Poor Febold! He now had no money, no team, no work! He went home, heartsick. Next morning when he went out where his mules lay dead, the ground was covered with animals—wolves, foxes, bears and skunks. They had been attracted by the dead mules and, coming up close, had seen the drifts of popcorn. They, too, had froze to death.

Well, to make a long story short, Febold got out his hunting knife and began to skin those animals. He was busy until late spring and made more money on the sale of the furs than he would have made farming in five years.

Febold was one of the first men west of the Mississippi to foresee the practical potentialities of the telegraph system. In fact, Febold originated one of the first, if not the first, telegraph system in the history of invention.

The Swede, a great fisherman, spent much of his time along the rivers. Because the Indian flunkeys on his home ranch often found it difficult to contact him, Febold devised a system of communication which, he felt, would save time and effort for all concerned. Equipped with a great ball of fish-line he tied one cord to his elbow and stretched it between his favorite fishing spot at the river and his home ranch. He and the Indians agreed upon a series of signals: one tug at the line meant one thing, two tugs meant another, and so on.

All went well for a while. Two tugs on the line, and Febold shouldered his rod and reel and headed for home. A tug or two from the Swede's end, and the Indian flunkeys came running to the river bank to see what he wanted.

One day a series of frenzied tugs at both ends of the line spelled trouble. Both Febold and the flunkeys came running to see what it was all about. They discovered that the disturbance was caused by a phoolphl bird, a species of sparrow which grew to gigantic proportions; the giant bird was attempting to pick up the string to build himself a nest.

97

Although Febold was frustrated by fickle fate, he did not abandon his project. Undaunted, he made changes in his basic invention but lacked a way to try it over distance. Since this was before the invention of wire, he restored to a heavily rosined string to carry the clicks made by his code sender. The string, stretched between the halves of two cocoanut shells, was pulled so tightly that it picked up all vibrations and transmitted them to the other end of the string.

All set to try out his invention, Febold invited a number of scientists and inventors to witness the demonstration. He hoped to sell his idea to the Union Pacific railroad.

The only thing that kept the apparatus from being a complete success was the autumn migration of woodpeckers. Just as the test began, a swarm of the birds swept from the sky, lighting on the building, the posts holding the string, and on nearby trees. Pecking for their dinner, they set up such an unearthly din that the sensitive string picked up the entire hullaballoo. Thinking they had been hoaxed, the group of experts stamped away.

The Swede wasn't going to give up his invention but other pressing matters caused him to shelve the idea. Before he got around to it again, an obscure artist named Samuel Morse had taken his brain child and reared it. Febold was heartbroken.

CHAPTER TEN

POST HOLES

If there was one thing which Febold wouldn't have around the place it was a mail order catalog. It was because Eldad Johnson's grandfather, out of sheer ornery cussedness, tried to beat Febold's record for digging post holes; Febold did—and still does—hold the record. But let's begin at the beginning.

When the Swede first came west in the early days there was no need of posts or post holes, because there were no cattle or cultivated land. Gradually, however, the pioneers felt the need for fences as the frontier pushed on across the Mississippi and into the Plains. They were familiar with the only two kinds of fences which had been used back east—the rail fence and the stone fence. Since there were neither trees nor stones on the Nebraska plains the early settlers were stumped. They would still be standing around sucking their thumbs if it hadn't been for Febold.

It was about this time that barbed wire was invented. Febold got busy and bought a few thousand miles of it. His problem

99

now was to get the posts to put the wire on. He accomplished this by digging post holes in the fall and letting them freeze all winter. Just before the spring thaw, he dug up the post holes and varnished them. After setting the posts securely in the ground, Febold strung the wire. In time the varnish wore off and left the post holes standing.

Bergstrom Stromberg declares that many of Febold's original post holes are still standing on his old home place on the Dismal River.

Herebold Farvardson takes exception to Stromberg's account. Herebold says that he has never seen a frozen post hole above ground. It seems that there were some on the old home place in the early days, but that Febold used them all up driving wells during the Year of the Great Heat. That was before the invention of the well-digger. Febold devised a unique scheme for digging wells: he drove a post hole into the ground and then another directly on top of it, and so on, until he hit water. A hundred foot post hole usually made a very fine well.

Luckily, it didn't really matter what became of the frozen post holes because it wasn't long before the pioneers shipped in real red cedar posts. The problem became the digging of the post holes. It was much too tedious to do the job by hand, and there was no machinery.

Again Febold came to the rescue. He recollected that the dismal sauger had a cousin, the happy auger, whose tail just suited his purpose.

The happy auger, also known as the snollygoster, was a peculiar creature. It looked rather like a kangaroo; it stood on its hind legs and had a long heavy tail which was easily the most peculiar part of this very peculiar animal. Its tail was shaped like a corkscrew, an instrument very common in those pre-bottle-cap days. Every time the happy auger sat down, it spun around on its tail and screwed it into the ground several feet. With this animal, Febold dug enough post holes daily to keep a hundred men busy sawing posts. After the auger was seated with its tail screwed in the ground, Febold sneaked up behind it and fired a six-shooter. The frightened creature jumped into the air twenty feet, leaving the prettiest post hole you ever saw.

Now Eldad Johnson's grandfather was one of those good-for-nothings who sit around all day back of the house looking through last year's mail order catalog. As long as he looked at the underwear section in the pink paper, he was happy and harmless. But when he got to the firearms section, in the green paper, he began to get crazy ideas. One day that goofy granddad of Eldad's ordered a machine gun from his favorite mail order house. When the gun arrived, he loaded it up and hid it in the barn.

The next morning, he got up before Febold and sneaked the happy auger away. He had decided that he and his new-fangled gun would beat Febold's record for digging post holes. Eldad's grandfather almost succeeded, but that was the last of the happy auger. When the machine gun began to fire the frightened creature leaped at every shot—in circles, in squares, in triangles, in right angles, quadrangles and rectangles. The auger at every leap left a perfect post hole. It finally jumped in a straight line directly for the Gulf of Mexico; the unhappy beast has never been seen since.

101

Old timers say that Febold caught Eldad Johnson's grandfather and made him fill up all the post holes. He didn't quite get them all filled, however, because he ran away and joined the Confederate Army. So if you find a post hole with no post, don't let anyone kid you when they tell you it's a gopher hole. Without a shadow of a doubt it's one of those post holes which Eldad Johnson's grandfather made with the happy auger and his mail order machine gun.

CHAPTER ELEVEN

THE WINTER OF THE PURPLE SNOW

Few people realize that the purple hue of the western prairies, always a picturesque feature of the colorful country, may be attributed directly to three factors—the Dirtyleg Indians, Indian Summer, and the Winter of the Purple Snow.

"Spring ain't really here," Bergstrom Stromberg always warns when the country enjoys one of its sunny days of deceptively early spring. "This is just one of them Indian Summer days the Weather Bureau had left over from last fall."

According to Bergstrom, it all started way back in the days when the Dirtyleg Indians petitioned Congress to continue Indian Summer all winter. Wall Street and the snowshoe interests, controlling a sufficient majority of the legislative body, effected the passage of a bill which provided for snowy weather. What happened was that somehow both bills went through and Congress, caught in a diplomatic dither, passed the buck by referring the matter to the Weather Bureau. The Weather Bureau was caught with too many warm days on its hands.

The officials were almost at their wits' end when Febold heard about the extra summer days. He asked that the government give him those days. He promised to slip a few in during February and March out on the Great Plains which were sparsely populated; the few settlers, he reasoned, would scarcely notice changes in the weather. The Weather Bureau, fed up with the Congressional setup, agreed gladly to Febold's plan.

Since Febold was only human, he probably played favorites. When a Sunday School class or a baseball team wanted a fine warm day Febold was glad to guarantee them one—for a slight consideration.

A few years later, however, during Lincoln's administration, Febold was so moved by the railsplitter-president's homespun humanity, that he realized his activities had been unscrupulous. Humiliated by his past iniquities, Febold gave his money to charity and returned the unused days to the Weather Bureau.

Congress, again faced with the weather issue, passed a law which provided for ten days of Indian Summer during February and March. These days were to be mixed up with the regular days and the ten were to be drawn by lot so no one could tell exactly when the days of warm weather were to occur. The proposal was found satisfactory.

It was during this year, while the Dirtylegs were having trouble with Congress, that the prairies turned purple. When they found that Congress had finally yielded to the Wall Street and snowshoe interests and refused to extend Indian Summer throughout the winter, prairie Indian tribes cursed until the air hung heavy with purple fog. Febold, as Indian agent, ordered a big snow from the Weather Bureau to clear the air and show

105

the unruly Indians that the government meant business. The snow lasted for days and days and the Indians, protesting profanely against the end of Indian Summer, made the air purple again. Febold ordered more snow and more snow until the Indians had to give up.

The snow, however, had turned purple. The great flakes which had drifted softly through the amethyst air retained their royal color. Throughout the winter, the prairies were lonely under a far-reaching blanket of deep purple snow. With the spring thaw, the sky-dyed snow vanished but the purple coloring stained the grass and sage brush of the plains, a constant reminder to the Indians of their misconduct.

During one of the famous blizzards in the early history of the state, Febold left his ranch house in mid-afternoon to milk his cattle. It had already grown dark and try as he might, even with his kerosene lantern in hand, the Swede could not find the errant animals.

The next morning Febold was convinced that his cattle had wandered into a gully and, trapped, were frozen to death by the extreme cold. He was amazed to see that the wind, during the night, had shaped the snow into the fantastic semblances of barnyard animals. There were icy images of cows, horses, chickens, rabbits, horses, pigs, and even a perfect snow man.

Always a frugal man, Febold decided that he could make some money by exhibiting these snow animals as a sort of phenomenon of nature. The Swede moved the animals into his yard and waited for spring to transport the images to the railroad depot from which he expected to freight them east.

Nebraska weather is a tricky thing. The next day turned warm and the snow began to thaw. Before he could get his snow images down into a cool cave, the snow melted. The animals became real animals; the snow man was—of course, you guessed it—Eldad Johnson's grandfather.

"There was just one thing peculiar," commented Bergstrom. "The rabbits didn't melt and when I was a little boy, it used to be fashionable for people to put 'em on their front lawns for every dog in town to bark at."

One winter Febold Feboldson nearly froze. A blizzard blew in from Canada and it snowed from early December to the first of March. Then a cold snap set in. It was so cold all the barbs were frozen from the barbed wire fences and the snow actually shrunk with cold. It was a common sight, according to Bergstrom Stromberg, to see Dirtyleg Indians walking around with their noses frozen off; several of the more unfortunate redskins even had their faces frozen off that winter.

On one particular morning it was so cold that Febold's breath froze the minute he exhaled it and he kept bumping into these huge bunches of frozen vapor. Deciding that his stock needed water, he went to the well but found his pump handle frozen solid. After thawing out the pump with a teakettle of boiling water, the Swede found the water in the pipe was frozen. Further investigation indicated that the water below that was also frozen.

When Febold tried to raise the frozen stream underground his superb strength caused one of the few earthquake shocks ever felt in the old Louisiana Purchase.

It is possible in these days of modern science, Bergstrom Stromberg observes, to hear the arrival of New Year's Day for four hours on the hour across the United States.

But before the invention of radio, one of the greatest New Year celebrations on record was the year Febold Feboldson carried New Year's greetings from the Governor of Maine to the Governor of California, and celebrated four New Years during his trip.

He started with a train which he himself engineered. Leaving New York at midnight, Febold's speed was so great at times that sections of the rails became red-hot, warped and had to be replaced. He was forced to leave his train at the Mississippi River. Wasting no time, he skated across the ice, hired a fast pony and when it was exhausted ran until he found a fast dog team which took him over the snow-covered prairies. He exchanged the dogs for a fast mountain burro which carried him across the Rockies. Febold finished up in sunny California astride a race horse whose foals later ran and won events at Santa Anita.

The wonderful part of Febold's fantastic journey, aside from the different means of transportation he employed, was the fact that he reached Cincinnati at 12 o'clock, arrived in Chicago at 12 o'clock, passed through Denver at 12 o'clock, and pulled into Sacramento at exactly 12 o'clock. He traversed the whole United

States, keeping within the changes of the four time zones—Eastern, Central, Mountain and Pacific—and celebrated the New Year in four cities en route.

This amazing feat has neither been duplicated nor equalled since.

CHAPTER TWELVE

ROCKS OF THE OX

The fate of Babe, Paul Bunyan's Blue Ox, has long been a subject of controversy. Lumbermen of the northwest declare that Babe died of eating red-hot stove lids, mistaking them for griddle cakes. Some persons, in an attempt to defame the memory of the mighty lumberman, whisper that Paul Bunyan butchered Babe during a long siege of hard times. As proof they point out the mastodon skeleton in the Smithsonian Institution and assure anyone who will listen that the bones are Babe's and not a mastodon's at all.

These stories, of course, are absurd. Only Bergstrom Stromberg knows what really became of Babe. Febold Feboldson, involved in the affair, handed the story down to his favorite grand-nephew.

It all happened during the Year of the Great Heat, when the temperature was never less than 150 degrees in the shade. That was the year it was so hot that dogs chasing cats walked. The Federal Government had drafted Febold and Paul Bunyan to fight Indians, especially the Dirtyleg tribe which had become bigger than their britches and were having an ornery streak. Instead of fighting Indians, however, Paul and Febold spent all their time trying to keep cool. After all, keeping cool is one of the requisites of Indian fighting.

About the Fourth of July, the heat became so unbearable that Paul, Febold and the Indians all took to the mountains. The mountains, closer to the sun, were hotter than the plains. The Indians dug caves in the sides of the mountains and finally escaped the heat. Remains of these cliff dwellings may be seen yet today pocking the mountain ranges of the Southwest.

Poor Babe couldn't make it. He reached the Rockies a few miles behind Paul and Febold but was so tired he lay down in the shadow of Pike's Peak and fell asleep. Looking back, while he straddled the Great Divide, Paul saw the Blue Ox.

"Suffering old saints and bleary-eyed fathers!" exploded the woodsman. "Look at Babe down there. We got to do something to cool off that there ox."

"That's right," Febold agreed. "When the sun comes up tomorrow morning he'll bake like a pie."

"In the name of the old holy mackinaw, what are we goin' to do?" Paul thoughtfully scratched his curly black beard with a young pine seedling.

"Well, we can't move the critter—that's sure as shootin'," the Swede observed.

"I got it!" shouted Paul, snapping his fingers. "Since we can't move Babe under that mountain, we gotta move the mountain over him."

111

No sooner said than done. Febold and the giant logger piled rocks around the Blue Ox until he was completely covered.

The next day the temperature skyrocketed another hundred degrees. Babe was roasted beneath the rocks. Not even Paul Bunyan or Febold Feboldson could cope with the sun's blistering rays.

Around Christmas, the Dirtyleg Indians skulked from their holes and began to forage in the snow for herbs buried beneath the blanket of white. They had had nothing to eat for three months or more. They found that the rocks with which the Ox was covered had retained the heat of the summer sun. The redskins began to carry the warm stones to their caves to heat their gloomy dwellings. Eventually, they discovered the carcass of the Blue Ox. With animal whoops of exaltation, the famished Indians fell upon the roast animal and devoured him completely. The rock pile, which they left strewn over the landscape at the foot of Pike's Peak, was named the Rocks of the Ox. Later, someone with more fantasy than fact in his esthetic soul, changed the name to the Garden of the Gods.

Paul Bunyan never quite recovered from his remorse that his enemies had devoured the remains of the Blue Ox. Febold and the lumberman had the last laugh, though. Babe proved too much for the Dirtyleg Indians. Shortly after their fabulous feast, every redskin writhed with indigestion. After squirming for hours in untold agony, every last Dirtyleg died. Paul Bunyan and Febold were awarded Distinguished Service Crosses by Congress for the extermination of the meanest Indian tribe west of the Mississippi River.

CHAPTER THIRTEEN

PRAIRIE PESTS

Whenever he hears his neighbors complain of corn borers, grasshoppers, or any of the other many infestations which beset the farmer, Bergstrom Stromberg reminds them of the pests endured by his great-uncle, Febold Feboldson, when the hardy pioneer first came to the state.

Rainy weather, one year, kept the Dismal River at near-flood state throughout the summer. When Febold irrigated, huge carp swam up the river and ate his corn while the Swede had to stand by helplessly doing nothing. He finally resorted to lassoing the fish and knocking them on the head with a hammer. The carp stopped bothering him in the daytime but nibbled his corn at night instead. Febold promptly stopped irrigating. Still the depredations continued.

One night he sat up to find out how the carp managed to get into his cornfield which was some distance from the river. The dew, he found, was so heavy that the fish swam into the field and nibbled the corn. Fireflies flitting among the tasseled stalks furnished light for the pests. Febold sensed the solution to his

problem. He spent the remainder of the night catching the fireflies and painting them black. His corn crop was saved.

The rabbits, too, reached unheard-of proportions. In the lean years rabbits grew so large and aggressive that they often attacked human beings. Febold recalled that once a jack rabbit chased him up a tree and kept him there for over a week, setting what was, for a long time, the tree-sitting record of the world.

Febold was a great one to make light of his misfortunes. In spite of adversity, he always managed to see the brighter side of things. This virtue contributed greatly to the success he made of his life.

The Swede once staked his entire fortune on a huge corn crop. Most of the summer it looked as if the yield would be bounteous, and Febold would become a rich man. Then the entire field was infested with corn borers. Most folks would have stood idly by and let their crop be ruined—but not Febold. He sat up night and day, and finally succeeded in teaching the borers to make cob pipes!

The Plains country was a hard country in which to get along in the old days. Only the fittest survived and, according to Bergstrom Stromberg, occasionally strange creatures resulted. The hardier specimens of lightning bugs furnished enough light that often the birds kept on flying after dark. Each bird had a pet bug to light its way, a situation which greatly upset the scheme of things. Complaints and a plea for help were sent by the newly-completed Union Pacific to the Federal Government. The lightning bugs and robins flew in front of the locomotives and often flagged the trains by the bright light reflected from the robin's breasts.

Another complaint from the Union Pacific reached the United States Government when birds pulled up all the spikes holding the rails to the ties. The birds, seeing the black heads of the spikes in the ties, assumed that they were worms. Shortly after they had pulled out and ate the spikes, a train from the east came along and the rails spread, causing a bad wreck. The government wrote Febold a scathing letter, in which they denounced him soundly for failing to keep the birds properly subdued. The Swede, his feelings greatly hurt, caught the birds and put "hobbles" on their beaks so that they couldn't open their mouths wide enough to pull any more spikes.

Some old-timers contend that Febold Feboldson was so tough that whenever a rattlesnake bit him the snake died. This is untrue, Bergstrom Stromberg declares, and quickly recalls the incident in which Febold was bitten by a whole nest of snakes while fighting his way through a swarm of mosquitoes to the Dismal River.

The Swede thought he was a goner for sure. His hands and feet swelled so greatly that he couldn't tell he had fingers or toes. When his eyes swelled shut, he decided it was all over, said his prayers and laid down to die. But he didn't die. He woke up the next morning feeling finer than ever. The swelling was gone, but still he couldn't see the Dismal River—because of the mosquitoes. The great heaps of insects were piled around him so high he couldn't see over the piles. The pests had sucked out all the snake poison and saved his life.

Bergstrom never heard of any snakes dying from biting Febold. A few instances have been reported where snakes bit him and broke their fangs but these injuries never proved fatal—to either the reptile or to the Swede.

Grasshopper swarms during the dry years of the thirties had the old-timers recalling similar plagues in previous years. But the Year the Grasshoppers Were Bad—undoubtedly the worst in the history of the state—was long before their time, Bergstrom Stromberg contends.

Grasshoppers were so thick that when they flew the sun was blotted out. Chickens went to their roosts and birds returned to their nests, thinking night had fallen.

Febold attempted to farm his huge ranch on the south bank of the Dismal River that year. One day when the grasshoppers ate the furrows as fast as Febold and his team could turn them, the Swede stopped the horses and walked over to the river for a drink of water. When he returned, Febold found the grasshoppers had eaten the team and harness, and were pitching the horseshoes to see which should have him.

Febold had the bright idea of importing wild turkeys to eat the 'hoppers. He made a trip to New England, snared a large number of these big birds and turned them loose on the Great Plains. The turkeys might have proved effective if the Indians had not found that the big birds made delightful meat. The redskins were so well pleased with their new repast that soon the turkeys disappeared entirely. The Indians encouraged the grasshoppers to return—which they continue to do yearly—thinking that Febold would again bring turkeys.

Reports that the Indians ate the turkeys are false, disputes Herebold Farvardson. This is what actually became of the birds, according to this great-nephew of Febold's:

The 'hoppers were so big and fierce that year that the turkeys themselves were hard pressed to keep from being devoured by the insects. Numerous instances of the feathers being eaten from the birds were reported. As the turkeys finally disappeared, authorities reached the conclusion that the Indians had eaten the birds or in their denuded condition they had caught cold and died.

The real facts behind the case—of which even the authorities who speculated about the birds' demise are unaware—are these, Farvardson contends:

The turkeys, after trying for three days to eat the 'hoppers, finally gave up and took flight. The 'hoppers, eager to rid the plains of the New England fowl, pursued the turkeys with great slashing jumps. The turkeys, thoroughly terrified, kept on the run so long that they did not even have time to stop and eat. The frenzied birds ran so long and so fast that they gradually shrank in size. Few people today realize that the game fowl called "quail" are descendants of the original New England wild turkey imported to the Great Plains by Febold Feboldson.

When he found that the turkeys were ineffective against the grasshoppers, Febold again wracked his brain to find a successful scheme to rid the country of the insect menace.

The wily Swede caught grasshoppers in a huge gunny sack but the ravenous insects ate their way out of the bag before Febold had time to tie it shut.

He then shot a herd of buffalo, took their hides and made another sack. The 'hoppers promptly ate their way out of this. Febold was so disappointed he was ready to quit. Then he heard that the pests had eaten a hundred Dirtyleg Indians in one day; he realized that he must find an effective way to rid the Plains of this scourge.

In a fit of infantile rage, Febold grabbed two handfuls of the grasshoppers and held them underwater in the Missouri River, wondering if the pests could be drowned. The fish ate them so fast that he nearly had his hands bitten off. This gave him an

118

idea. Febold caught a number of the bigger fish and crossed them with Canadian geese. He raised a flock of these winged creatures, then turned them loose on the prairies. In less than a week the land was rid of the 'hoppers, and the flying fish had become a bigger nuisance than the grasshoppers had been.

Febold then imported timber wolves to catch the fish. And to keep the timber wolves happy, the Swede planted the prairies with more cottonwoods; the prairie was no longer a prairie but a cottonwood wood.

The grasshoppers would have stayed exterminated and everybody would have lived happily ever after if Southern planters had not wanted more cotton and more slave states. A group of Southerners hired Febold to experiment with cottonwoods and sent him a small army of Negro cotton pickers.

The first week was a big success. The Negroes picked the cotton off the cottonwoods as far up as they could reach. Because it took too much time to move step-ladders from tree to tree, Febold brought the cotton within reach of the pickers by bending the trees double and sticking their top branches in the ground. The Southerners thought Febold was just about the smartest guy they had ever seen. The next year, however, they piped a different tune. When they came back in the spring, the cottonwood trees had grown back into the ground and completely disappeared.

This incident had a great deal more to do with the cause of the Civil War than historical authorities admit, reveals Bergstrom Stromberg. Until now, he continues, the Cottonwood Conspiracy has remained one of the "hush-hush" scandals which never appear in the pages of school children's history books.

The timber wolves, too, felt the loss of the cottonwood trees. Since they had no homes, the animals attempted to migrate from the Great Plains. They were stopped on the east by the Mississippi, on the south by the Rio Grande, on the west by the Rockies, and on the north by the Canadian Northwest Mounted Police. Finally, they returned to the Great Plains to die of homesickness for their native woods.

Luckily, Febold was kind to animals and couldn't endure the sight of the timber wolves' suffering. He tried to explain to the wolves that the trees were just under ground. He dug up a few to prove it. As soon as the wolves caught on to the idea, they began to dig frantically among the buried trees. Because of the energy spent in digging, each succeeding generation was stunted, becoming smaller than the one before it. Today they are only a fraction of their former size and are commonly known as "prairie dogs."

CHAPTER FOURTEEN

CALIFORNIA, THIS WAY OUT

Febold's last public appearance was in Omaha a number of years ago, where he attended a practice shoot in which other pioneers and trappers competed for prizes. Because someone maliciously took the shells from his rifle, Febold failed to win. In the noise and din of the shooting, he did not notice that he was clicking an empty gun.

Thinking he had succumbed to buck fever, Febold came away disheartened and unhappy, left the Great Plains for California.

Whether Febold went to California for good or only for a visit, no one perhaps will ever know.

Bergstrom Stromberg thinks he has gone only for a visit. Eldad Johnson, whose grandfather accompanied Febold in many of his escapades, is probably of the same opinion. In Bergstrom's presence, however, he always takes the opposite view and gives vent to his exasperation with his native prairies and his own suppressed desire to go to California. All one needs to start them off is to ask in a casual manner when Febold is coming back.

"He ain't never comin' back!" Eldad snaps in a voice that is anything but casual.

"How do you know he ain't?" Bergstrom will ask.

"Because any man as smart as Febold would know enough to stay away from this here man-killin', God-forsaken country," Eldad answers. "Why, if you ain't burned up by drouths or winds hotter'n the hinges o' Hades, you're frozen out by blizzards and hail storms, or you're et alive by grasshoppers an' speculators an' politicians—"

"Now, wait a minute," Bergstrom tries to stop Eldad.

"No, sir, I won't wait a minute! I'm goin' to have my say," the other insists, stubborn as a calf learning to drink out of a bucket. "Febold did his gol-derndest to make this country fit for a white man to live in, an' he couldn't do it! And by jumpin' jiminy crickets, if Febold couldn't do it, they ain't nobody can!"

"Well, now, look here—"

"No, sir, it can't be done, and I don't blame Febold one bit fer packin' up bag an' baggage an' goin' off to Californy with the rest o' the sensible people."

"Whoa, there! Whoa, now!" Bergstrom finally gets Eldad stopped. "Ain't you bein' just a little strong? You want to remember, my great-uncle Febold ain't no lily-livered cake-eater like some folks I could name."

"Now you needn't look at me when you say that."

"I ain't lookin' at you. These here plains is tough country, and it takes tough people to live here. Febold ain't backed out yet, and don't you fergit it!"

"Just the same he did go to Californy," Eldad points out, unconvinced, then adds quickly before Bergstrom can come to his great-uncle's defense. "He ain't back yet—an' he never will be. I'd bust my hame-string myself to git out there—if I had the money. No, sir, I know Febold was a tough feller an' liked a good big job. But he was smart, too—smart enough to know when he was licked!"

"Licked!" This thrust always brings a dangerous gleam into Bergstrom's eyes. "Why, he ain't licked—he ain't even begun to fight!"

"He ain't, eh?"

"No, sir, he ain't." Bergstrom promises, "Why, all them tricks and little shenanigans he used to pull in the early days won't hold a candle to what he's gonna do when he gets back from Californy."

"Aw-w-w-w, go on with you."

"You just wait an' see. Say, do you really want to know why Febold went to Californy?"

"Want to know? Cripes, I do know! So does anybody else with a lick o' sense," Eldad explodes. "He went to get away from here so he could enjoy his old age without fightin' this cussed country all the time."

"You talk like you fell on your head," Bergstrom observes dryly.

"Why, do you know what I heard?" Eldad ignores Bergstrom's remark. "I heard Febold was a bartender down in Tia Juana till he made some money on the horses at Santa Anita. Then he bought some steamships tradin' with China or someplace. Heard he had a fruit farm out there someplace, an' was playin' in the movin' pitchers for a while, too."

"Why, Eldad Johnson, I'm surprised at you," counters Berg-

strom. "You know Febold's too big a man to monkey 'round with things like horse races an' steamships an' fruit farms an' movin' pitchers! You know what he went to Californy for?"

"What for?"

"To study."

"Study what?" Eldad asks, always in a tone of utmost contempt.

"Irrigation and forestry," Bergstrom always replies. "Science, you know. Things is done different now. When Febold gets back, he's gonna put water and trees on these here plains—no foolin'."

"Can't be done," Eldad says flatly, shaking his head.

Nebraska Strong Men

by Louise Pound

Legends of strong men are, of course, no new or rare or purely American phenomena. The literature and lore of many races exhibit tales of the supernormally mighty. There are stories of their birth, rearing, precocity, and their marvellous achievements, such as their feats of lifting, uprooting trees, victories over antagonists, or rescues of victims.[1] Ajax of Homer's *Iliad* is a man of brute strength and courage. So is the mythical Hercules, of whose superhuman power tall tales are told, one of which was that on occasion he relieved Atlas by supporting the world. Another strong man was Samson, the Hebrew judge whose strength was liquidated by Delilah. Another was Beowulf who "had the strength of thirty men in his hand-grip." In American lore there are Kwasind, the strong man of Longfellow's *Hiawatha*, John Henry, the Negro steel driver who "died with his hammer in his hand," Paul Bunyan of the Northern woods, and there are those two up-to-date muscle men, Tarzan the "giant," who springs from tree to tree—these always miraculously at hand and the branches unfailingly holding and concealing him—and there is Superman.

Febold Feboldson

Nebraska, too, has its offering of strong men. There are at least three of whom stories have been current: Febold Feboldson,

---

[1] See Stith Thompson's *Motif-Index of Folk-Literature* (III, 142-150), 1934, for instances of legendary strong men among the Celts, Norse, Dutch, Italians, Hindus, American Indians, etc.

Antoine Barada, and Moses Stocking. Of these Febold looms largest. He has achieved by this time something of a bibliography as a folk hero. Originally the protagonist of a number of yarns, by known authors, in Gothenburg, Nebraska, newspapers, Febold made his début before the general public in an article "Paul Bunyan and Febold" published by Paul Robert Beath in the *Prairie Schooner* (VI, 59-61) in 1932. Mr. Beath's yarn narrates "How Paul Bunyan and Febold Became Acquainted." It is supposed to be told by Bergstrom Stromberg, who is "over 90" and who is a "grand-nephew of Febold"; "Bergstrom remembers both men well." Febold's deeds were selected and written up or edited by Mr. Beath for the Nebraska Folklore pamphlets of the Writers' Project of 1937. Next a story, "How Febold Cured the Coyote Plague with Whimpering Whingdings," was included in Carl Carmer's *Hurricane's Children* (1937). Then came Anne Malcomson's *Yankee Doodle's Cousins* (1941) giving Febold added recognition. A Febold story is to be included in B. A. Botkin's *Treasury of American Folklore,* announced as in preparation. There is an unpublished volume, a compilation of Febold tales with a foreword by Frederick Christensen, which I have seen but which is not yet available to the public [*Febold Feboldson: Tall Tales from the Great Plains,* compiled by Paul R. Beath, Lincoln: University of Nebraska Press, 1948].

Mr. Carmer's headnote to the Febold tale he includes in *Hurricane's Children* reads:

> Febold Feboldson is a bit younger than most of the giants in this book but he is just as strong and just as smart. News of him and his adventures has been traveling about Nebraska from Lincoln and Gothenburg to David City and Red Cloud, Wahoo, and Prairie Home, North Star and Horsefoot. Perhaps he is one of Paul Bunyan's Swedish lumberjacks who has started out on his own in Nebraska.

The "Paul Bunyan Twenty-Five Years After" of Gladys J. Haney [2] cites Febold as "among the best known folk heroes."

---

2 *JAFL*, LV, July-September, 1942.

In view of his rapid rise to celebrity, it seems in place to record Febold's history before it is forgotten. I have been interested for years in Nebraska lore. Masses of materials have been sent me or gathered for me. Various studies made by graduate students are available in printed form: for example, *Proverbial Lore in Nebraska* by Louise Snapp and *Signs, Omens and Portents in Nebraska Folklore* by Margaret Cannell,[3] *Nebraska Folk Cures* by Pauline Black,[4] and Florence Maryott treated "Nebraska Counting Out Rhymes" in the *Southern Folklore Quarterly*.[5] B. A. Botkin's notable *American Play-Party Song* took final form and was printed in Nebraska.[6] And considerable folklore and folksong material is at hand which has not yet been published. But never, in more than a quarter of a century, has anything been contributed to me about Febold. Those persons I have questioned who come from Gothenburg, Wahoo, North Platte, and Lincoln testified promptly that they had never heard of him. The stories of Febold published in the Writers' Project pamphlet do not name the tellers or give place and date. They are not "documented" in scholarly fashion. The fact is that Febold, the prairie hero, originated as a flight of fancy, patterned after Paul Bunyan, and he owes most of his fame, I think, to Mr. Paul R. Beath, who, though not his creator, has spun many stories about him and floated him into fame. Those who have been most closely associated with the Febold stories, men such as L. C. Wimberly of the *Prairie Schooner*, Frederick Christensen, J. Harris Gable, and Paul Beath himself readily admit the success of the venture and that Febold gained national prominence as a folk hero with surprising quickness.

The character Febold, the strong man, and his name seem to have been created by Wayne Carroll, a local lumber dealer, who wrote a column under the name of Watt Tell in the now defunct Gothenburg, Nebraska, *Independent*.[7] This series began

---

3 *University of Nebraska Studies in Language, Literature and Criticism,* 1933.

4 *Ibid.,* 1935.

5 December, 1937.

6 Lincoln: *University of Nebraska Studies,* 1937.

7 This is the testimony of Don Holmes to Paul R. Beath.

about 1923. Later Carroll used Febold in advertising that he wrote for his lumber company. Febold could never have been made a lumber hero like Paul Bunyan, for there are no trees on the great plains. So he became a hero wrestling with the adversities of the prairie region, tornadoes, droughts, extreme heat and cold, Indians, politicians, and disease. Later matter, concerning Febold, from the pens of Carroll and Don Holmes and other contributors, appeared in the Gothenburg *Times,* 1928-33, and sporadically since.

Carroll may have had in mind for his creation of Bergstrom Stromburg, the fabulous person usually cited as relating the Febold tales, a real person, Olof Bergstrom, who founded Gothenburg, Nebraska. He is sometimes said to have founded Stromsburg also, probably through confusion with his brother who located there. Olof Bergstrom was a pioneer leader of immigrant Swedes into Nebraska, who had a somewhat hectic career and stories of whom, Mr. Beath says, were current when he was a boy.

The Febold stories "caught on" about 1928. After Wayne Carroll, not only did Don Holmes write them but contributions began to come in from readers of the *Times.* From this mass Mr. Beath gleaned the stories which he wove into his version of Febold's exploits which appeared in the Nebraska folklore pamphlet and earlier in the Omaha *World-Herald* and the *Prairie Schooner* (1932). All the material has now been turned over to B. A. Botkin, who is in charge of the Archive of American Folksong in the Library of Congress at Washington.

But for Paul R. Beath I fear that Febold might have died with the early newspaper yarns about him, yarns of the extravagant type liked by newspaper writers and readers in the later nineteenth and early twentieth century, and usually pretty ephemeral. Mr. Beath was educated at the University of Illinois and at Columbia. Formerly of Gothenburg, he is now an attorney for the government at Washington. I first knew of him as a contributor of interesting matter concerning the living language to *American Speech.* He writes on folk topics and is a lover of folklore. In answer to inquiries from me he wrote:

I first became aware of Febold when stories of him were appearing in the Gothenburg *Times*. About this time I read James Stevens' *Paul Bunyan* (1925). I recognized the resemblance of Febold to Paul. . . . It was during this period that I started contributing an occasional story to the *Times*. . . . My stories were mostly adaptations of those I heard about town, yarns of various types, not however Febold yarns. These I elaborated and embellished to fit Febold and what I conceived to be his character, i.e., an indomitable Swedish pioneer who could surmount any difficulty. As a boy and young man I worked my way as a night clerk in a hotel in Gothenburg where I heard literally thousands of stories told by traveling salesmen and other garrulous wayfarers. I suppose I received clues to many of the stories from this ever-flowing stream.

As a contemporary instance of the type of yarning to which he refers, Mr. Beath tells that when he was traveling by bus from Schuyler to Grand Island, Nebraska, recently, a passenger exclaimed that he saw a rabbit. Another passenger promptly said, "That is no rabbit but a Kansas grasshopper." Asked how he knew, he answered that rabbits are as big as coyotes in the Nebraska region. This bantering and yarning was continuing when Mr. Beath left the bus at Grand Island. His testimony concerning Febold ended with the remarks:

I cannot let this opportunity go by without having my say about that school of folklorists who try to find the origins of stories in the race or in some mythical super-personality, some "geist" lurking in the twilight. This seems to me all poppycock. Stories are told, even concocted, by individuals for the entertainment of individuals. Every story that was ever told was told by an individual and his individual artistry or lack of it is apparent. Every Febold story has been told or written by an individual and I know at least six of these tellers personally— and it has been put together out of the narrative material already in the teller's head.

So much for Febold, the folk hero. Folklore is folklore, whatever its origin, and Febold now belongs to folklore. But it is the lore of the literary class, the lore of educated lovers of lore, rather than of the sub-literary, the less educated strata usually thought of as the "folk" of "folklore." The same may be true, or is true, of Paul Bunyan. Lore of Paul is now folklore, but it is the folklore of the reading class. There may have been an *ur*-Paul Bunyan, possibly a real person about whom stories centered; but the legendary Paul neither seems to have emerged from the woodsmen nor to be very current among them, except as handed down from above.

Since Paul Bunyan is so obviously the progenitor of Febold, it may be in place to digress a little concerning him here. Tales of him are said by Esther Shephard (1924) to have originated even earlier than the 1860's and to have been at their height in the 1880's and '90's, though some of her tales involve materials and inventions (as a parachute and pipelines) that did not exist in those decades.

Mr. Carleton C. Ames of the River Falls State College, Minnesota, writing on "Paul Bunyan—Myth or Hoax?" in the *Minnesota History Magazine*,[8] does not accept the tales of Paul Bunyan as indigenous folklore, i.e., as yarns actually spun by the shanty boys of logger camps in Wisconsin, Minnesota, and Michigan. His father, he says, was raised in an atmosphere of logging camps and his grandfather spent most of his active life in the logging industry. They had never heard of Paul Bunyan nor did those old-timers with whom Mr. Ames had informal conversations, men from camps representing Minnesota, Wisconsin, Maine, also some from Canada, including Scandinavians. Not one had ever heard Paul Bunyan mentioned. Nor does his name appear in Franz Rickaby's authentic *Ballads and Songs of the Shanty Boy* (1926), gathered at first hand from loggers, nor, I may add, is there a single reference to Paul Bunyan among the songs, older, later, and contemporary, of Maine woodsmen, gathered at first hand by Mrs. Eckstorm and Miss Smyth in their *Minstrelsy of Maine* (1927). Moreover (this too was pointed out by Mr. Ames), Stewart H. Holbrook in *Holy Old Mackinaw* (1938), a history of the logging industry, in a chapter headed "Around the Barrel Staves," states, "legends grew out of these bunkhouse discourses—not the made-up tales of Paul Bunyan

---

[8] XXI, 55-58. 1940.

but tales of actual men." Apparently, Esther Shephard and many others since accepted the tales at face value as emerging from the mid-nineteenth century loggers themselves. Another researcher who, like Carleton Ames, believes that the Paul Bunyan legends did not come up out of the woods and logging camps but were superimposed upon them, is Dr. M. M. Quaife of Wayne University, Detroit, Michigan, who testifies [9] that "after tackling the subject" he came to the same conclusion as Mr. Ames.

The real impetus given the Paul Bunyan legends seems to have been commercial. They first gained currency in the publications of the Red River Lumber Company of Minnesota, which started giving Paul Bunyan stories in 1914. At that date Paul was unknown to the general public and to the distributors and sawmill people. Whether Paul was an earlier or a new creation (an unsigned note in the *Minnesota History Magazine* cites a solitary instance of an individual over 80 who thought he remembered the existence of Paul Bunyan stories as far back as the 1870's), it seems certain that America in general would not have heard of him but for W. B. Laughead, who may be termed the real promoter of the yarns and who was no doubt the creator of many of them. Mr. Laughead was the author of a booklet on the marvellous exploits of Paul Bunyan, published by the Red River Lumber Company in 1922. Laughead said he first heard of Paul Bunyan in the region about Bemidji, Minnesota, in 1900. Whether he found earlier tall tales (an *ur*-Paul) and elaborated and added to them and created others, or was in most respects Paul's sponsor, I do not know. In any case Paul, floated commercially, now belongs to folklore. Witness writers like Stuart Chase who stated in 1925 that the Paul Bunyan stories are "a golden chunk of almost pure primitive literature." Lucy L. Hazard said Paul Bunyan is now "of the stature of the nation," this in 1927. James Cloyd Bowman in 1941 termed the Paul Bunyan tales "the most fundamentally American of all our folklore." No, there is no doubt that Paul won wide accep-

---

[9] *Minnesota History Magazine*, XXI, 176-178. 1940.

tance as a folk hero genuinely of folk emergence.[10] By the middle of this century, however, theories of his origin and the origin of the tales attributed to him have been given up.[11]

For later Febold matter see my review in *Nebraska History*, XXX, 77-80, of Beath's *Tall Tales of the Great Plains* (University of Nebraska Press, 1948), and especially the dependable summary "The Febold Feboldson Legends" by Robert F. Chamberlain, in *Nebraska History*, XXXIII (June, 1952), 95-102.

I have omitted account of the nature and content of the Febold tales, offspring of the Paul Bunyan tales, for they are available in print in various places. They are of much the same extravagant character as the Bunyan stories. For example, one

---

[10] See Gladys J. Haney's bibliography, *JAFL*, LV, July-September, 1942. J. Frank Dobie, 1925, seems to have been skeptical concerning Paul Bunyan.

[11] Since this article was written I have heard from Mr. W. R. Laughead, who now represents the California Plant of the Red River Lumber Company at Westwood, Lassen County, in that State. His tall tales of Paul Bunyan seem to have been the first to appear in print. I have a copy from him of the first booklet of the Company on Paul Bunyan, issued in 1914. Newspaper contributions concerning Paul seem to have followed, much as for Febold. Esther Shephard's book came in 1924 and James Steven's in 1925. The part of Mr. Laughead's letter responding to my inquiries concerning Paul Bunyan is of especial interest to folklorists:

"Where and how Paul Bunyan started no one seems to know, although there is evidence that he was known in Eastern States, where logging was at its height before the Great Lakes period of the industry. The material in the 1922 Red River book *Paul Bunyan and His Blue Ox* was gathered from many sources. It started with what I remembered from Minnesota logging camps (1900-1908). I then picked up odds and ends from letters we received and from columns that ran in various newspapers, in the Seattle *Star* by Lee J. Smits, the Portland *Oregonian* by DeWitt L. Hardy, and others. Correspondence to the *American Lumberman* also provided clues. Most of this had appeared between the publication of our first booklet in 1914 and the trade journal advertisements we ran 1914-1916, and the compilation of *Paul Bunyan and His Big Blue Ox*, 1922.

"At original sources (conversation of loggers and other workers) I never heard the narrative form. Even the extemporaneous additions came as off-hand mention of events and Paul's inventions, as if referring to well-known facts. My own 'invention' included names of characters, 'Babe,' 'Brimstone Bill,' 'Johnny Inslinger,' 'Sourdough Sam,' etc. . . . My writing has been almost entirely advertisements."

On the whole, the testimony of Mr. Laughead tends to strengthen the assumption that the floating of Paul Bunyan stories was commercial and that Mr. Laughead played much the same role for Paul that P. R. Beath was to play for Febold.

tale mentions that strange animal the "hodag," which is taken directly from the Paul Bunyan stories. And I shall treat the other two Nebraska strong men more briefly.

Antoine Barada

The Writers' Project pamphlet of the Nebraska W.P.A., 1937, characterized Antoine Barada as "the strongest man who ever roamed the shores of the Missouri River." The headnote prefixed to stories of him in the pamphlet ranks him as "second only to Febold as a legendary or mythical character." Antoine has a very different history from Febold. There is evidence that a person of that name really lived, though the stories of his parentage do not agree. The account in the pamphlet states that Antoine Barada "was the son of Count Michael Barada, a gay Parisian, and Laughing Water, a pretty Omaha maiden. Since she was of the Omaha tribe, the Count and his wife resided in Thurston County, Nebraska. Antoine spent his later years on the reservation with them. He died in 1866 and was buried beside his wife in Richardson County at the little village of Barada, which was named in his honor." This was the parentage ascribed to Antoine by Robert Maher, who wrote of his remarkable deeds in the *Sunday Journal and Star* of Lincoln, Nebraska, June 14, 1936. Maher's account may have been used by the Writers' Project authors, or the two accounts may have been derived from the same source.

Mari Sandoz, best known as the author of *Old Jules* (1935) and *Crazy Horse* (1942), who was employed for some time in the office of the Secretary of the Nebraska State Historical Society and who served as Assistant Editor of the *Nebraska History* magazine, is my chief informant concerning Antoine. She testifies that she knew stories of him when she was a child. He was a half-breed, she says, the son of Michael Barada, who "was supposed to be of royal connections in Spain. . . . The town of Barada in Richardson County was named after Michael. . . . Around 1934, while I was working at the State Historical Society, a letter came in seeking information on the Barada family, to settle as I recall now, an estate. Whether

133

this was another of the recurring Spanish inheritance hoaxes I don't know now. . . . There was also a Michael Barada in the Custer County region for a while, I'm told."

Still another statement, this the earliest printed statement I have, appears in *Nebraska Place-Names,* compiled in 1924 and published in the *University of Nebraska Studies in Language, Literature, and Criticism* (1925). This account of leading town-names in the state was made by Lilian Fitzpatrick, A.M., with some assistance from her father, Professor T. J. Fitzpatrick of the Botanical Department, an experienced place-name researcher. The entry reads: "Barada. This place is situated in Barada precinct and it and the precinct were named after one of the first settlers, Antoine Barada (1807-1887), a French-Omaha half-breed whose wife was a French woman. He named the village after himself. His descendants still live in the vicinity."

The name Barada is on the certified copy of the census of half-breeds listed in volume XVI, p. 40, of the *Nebraska History* magazine. In volume I, page 2, a Michael Barada is said to have been elected a "sentinel of the Union Club" in 1863, the Civil War period.

All in all, whether Antoine Barada the half-breed was Spanish-Indian as suggested by the name Barada which sounds Spanish, or French-Indian as suggested by Antoine, and whether the town was named after him or after Michael Barada, he seems to have been a real person, perhaps some one of unusual strength and of various adventures. In the legends about him he pulls out a big boat stranded in the sandbars, picks up a 400 pound boulder, and does similar feats. Miss Sandoz recalls of him:

Antoine Barada was a hurry-up man, always rushing, rushing, can't wait for anything. One time he got tired of watching a pile driver working along the Missouri with the hammer making the up-down, up-down, the driver yelling "Git up! Git up! Whoa! Back! Back! Whoa!" and then all of it over again and the piling going down maybe a half inch. So Antoine he picked up the damned thing in his bare hand, throws it high and far so it lights clear over the Missouri where it bounce and bounce leaving ground tore up for miles and miles and making what the greenhorns call "Breaks of the Missouri." But at last it stop and if you dig down in them high ridges you find it is the damned pile driver with grass growing over him, a little poor soil, you understand, but it seems to satisfy them that ain't never crossed the Missouri and don't know better. When Antoine had disposed of the Johny Jumper hammer he sees that the piling that is left stands a mile higher than the rest, so he gives it a lick with his fist and it pop down into ground so deep it strike buried lake, the water flying out like from bung hole fifty feet high and like to drown out the whole country if Antoine he did not sit on the hole first.

Miss Sandoz says that she "grew up on the Barada stories as told by half-breeds around Pine Ridge." They were brought there, she suspects, by the Ruleaus and other families who used to live on what is called the Breed Strip in southeast Nebraska, and in the early 1900's still had relatives to visit there.

Moses Stocking

Concerning the stories of my third and last Strong Man figuring in Nebraska legend, Moses Stocking, my only informant so far is Miss Sandoz. She reports:

A rather neglected group of strong man stories in which mind rules over mere brawn are the Moses Stocking stories. These were floating around Western Nebraska in my childhood, always about a man in Eastern Nebraska who ran sheep. I don't remember many of these and know of no place where they reached print. All the great plant and animal stories were fastened to him, such as the squash vines that grew so fast they wore the squashes out dragging them over the ground. Or the corn that grew so tall a boy was sent up the stalk to measure it and was never heard from again except that they know he's still alive because they sell a trainload of corn cobs every year from around the foot of the Stocking corn stalk, thrown down by the boy, who must be a gray-haired man now because the bird nests found in the corn leaves are made with grey hair.

There was also a story of how Stocking went into sheep:

He had an acre of bottom land broke (Stocking never did any of the work himself, you understand), and because it was late he couldn't sow anything himself except a few turnips. The seed was bad and only five plants came up, one in each corner and one in the middle; but they grew pretty well. The corner ones squashed and flattened of course, being so close together, and too puny for any real use, although they hauled one of them to the top of a hill somewhere along the Platte and when it was hollowed out and the wind dried it, it was used as a military academy and did very well for years to house the boys. Another one from the corners was used for the railroad depot at Omaha, since there would be only temporary use for a depot there. The other two corner turnips were wasted, as I recall, but the center one was worth saving and from it grew the Stocking fortune. After walking around it once and coming back footsore and with cockleburrs in his beard, old Moses took the train for Chicago and bought up all the sheep at the stock-market and for the next month there was a stream wide as the Missouri of sheep coming across Iowa to the Stocking place. They started eating at the turnip where Moses blasted a hole and they lived there fat and sung all winter, not having to go into the blizzard cold at all, just eating the pulp out, the shell making a shelter for the sheep that were worth enough to keep Jay Cook afloat for a whole year after he really was broke, only the public didn't know it.

These yarns testify to the intellectual rather than to the physical strength of Moses Stocking, but Miss Sandoz recalled that old timers told also how the old fellow lifted wagons out of the mud and did similar strong-man feats.

Miss Sandoz added, when recounting Moses Stocking stories, that she believes there really was a Moses Stocking who lived in eastern Nebraska, although the stories she knew of him floated about western Nebraska. She is right in her belief. A Moses Stocking existed. He was a pioneer of ability and considerable distinction who lived on a farm in Saunders County, Nebraska, in the Ashland-Wahoo region. He was a charter member of the Nebraska Historical Society. His Autobiography, telling of his difficult and venturesome life, was printed in the first volume of the *Transactions and Reports* of the Nebraska Historical Society, pp. 128-137, 1885. He was a member of the Fine Stock Breeders' Association and of the State Board of Agriculture. In the column reprinting, day by day, news from old files of the Nebraska *State Journal,* I found in the *Evening Journal* for July 22, 1943, under the heading "Sixty Years Ago Today," the entry "Moses Stocking of Eldred, Saunders County, was the most extensive wool grower in the state. He had 1,500 sheep."

This exhausts my knowledge to date of Nebraska Strong Men in legend. The Nebraska heroes, surviving into the present in print or orally, are obviously not "sissies," or "cream puffs," or in contemporary jargon, "panty-waists." They are genuine strong men. Two of the sets of tales seem to have become attached to or centered about real persons. In this there is no novelty. To recall but a few prototypes of Antoine Barada and Moses Stocking, the emperors Alexander the Great, Charlemagne, and Friedrich Barbarossa were historic personages about whom tall tales gathered and were handed on.

Read before the Western Folklore Conference at the University of Denver, July 16, 1943. Reprinted from the *Southern Folklore Quarterly,* VII (September, 1943), 133-143.